THE ART AND ARCHITECTURE OF
ANCIENT GREECE

THE ART AND ARCHITECTURE OF
ANCIENT GREECE

AN ILLUSTRATED ACCOUNT OF CLASSICAL GREEK BUILDINGS, SCULPTURES
AND PAINTINGS, SHOWN IN 250 GLORIOUS PHOTOGRAPHS AND DRAWINGS

NIGEL RODGERS

southwater

This edition is published by Southwate
an imprint of Anness Publishing Ltd
Blaby Road, Wigston, Leicestershire LE18 4SE
Email: info@anness.com
Web: www.southwaterbooks.com; www.annesspublishing.com

Anness Publishing has a new picture agency outlet for images for publishing, promotions or advertising. Please visit our website www.practicalpictures.com for more information.

Publisher: Joanna Lorenz
Editor: Joy Wotton
Designers: Nigel Partridge, Adelle Morris
Illustrations and maps: Peter Bull Art Studio, Vanessa Card, Anthony Duke
Production Controller: Christine Ni

ETHICAL TRADING POLICY
Because of our ongoing ecological investment programme, you, as our customer, can have the pleasure and reassurance of knowing that a tree is being cultivated on your behalf to naturally replace the materials used to make the book you are holding. For further information about this scheme, go to www.annesspublishing.com/trees

PUBLISHER'S NOTE
Although the advice and information in this book are believed to be accurate and true at the time of going to press, neither the authors nor the publisher can accept any legal responsibility or liability for any errors or omissions that may be made.

Previously published as part of a larger volume, *The Ancient Greek World*

PICTURE ACKNOWLEDGEMENTS
The Art Archive: /Gianni Dagli Orti 2, 5.2, 15b, 23b, 24t, 22tl, 24t, 26t, 27t, 28b, 33tl, 34t, 42–3, 44t, 45t, 50b, 51bl and br, 64b, 65t; /Archaeological Museum Spina Ferrara/ Alfredo Dagli Orti 5.5, 104–5, 115t; /National Archaeological Museum Athens/ Gianni Dagli Orti 75t, 76r, 77tl, 78tl, 79tr, 80tl, 86tl, 92t, 96tl, 97t, 98m, 111; /Musée du Louvre Paris/ Gianni Dagli Orti 100tr; /Galerie Berko Louvre des Antiquaires/ Gianni Dagli Orti 6–7; /Bibliothèque des Arts Décoratifs Paris/Gianni Dagli Orti 17bl; /Archaeological Museum Chora Greece/Gianni Dagli Orti 21b; /Stephanie Colasanti 23b; /Archaeological Museum Corinth/ Gianni Dagli Orti 28t; /Alfredo Dagli Orti 44b; /Museo Nazionale Reggio Calabria/Gianni Dagli Orti 53bm, 101tr; /Agora Museum Athens/ Gianni Dagli Orti 57b; /Olympia Museum Greece/ Gianni Dagli Orti 76l, 90tl; /Archaeological Museum Cherchel Algeria/Gianni Dagli Orti 86b; /Musée Archéologique Naples/Alfredo Dagli Orti 88t; /Museo Capitolino Rome/ Alfredo Dagli Orti 91br, 125t; /Museo Nazionale Taranto/ Gianni Dagli Orti 94tr; /Museo di Villa Giulia Rome/Gianni Dagli Orti 110tl; /Eleusis Museum Greece/Gianni Dagli Orti 110tr; /Archaeological Museum Florence/Gianni Dagli Orti 112tl; /Archaeological Museum Ferrara/ Alfredo Dagli Orti 114b; /Musée d'archéologie méditérranéenne, Marseilles/Gianni Dagli Orti 115br; /Galleria degli Uffizi Florence/ Alfredo Dagli Orti 121b;
The Ancient Art & Architecture Collection: 5.1, 8 l and r, 14–15, 16tl, 17t, 18t and b, 20b, 21t, 22tr, 24b, 25tl, tr and b, 26b, 29, 30tl and tr, 31t and b, 32t and b, 33b, 34b, 35b, 36t and b, 37t and b, 38t, 39t and b, 40 t and b, 41t, 46 t, m and br, 47b, 49b, 53tl, 56t, 58t and b, 59b, 60t and b, 62t, 63t, 64t, 65b, 66tl and tr, 67t, 68t, 69t, 70t and b, 71t and b, 74b, 75b, 79bl, 80br, 82l, 83r, 84 t and b, 85l and r, 87t and b, 89b, 90b, 91t, 93, 94tl, 95l and r, 98t, 99t, 101b, 106t and b, 107t and b, 108b, 109, 112b, 113t and b, 114t, 119t and bl, 122b, 124t and b; /C.M. Dixon 5.4, 46bl, 72–3; /Prisma 77b, 103t; /R. Ashworth 51t; /G. Tortali 61b; /Ronald Sheridan 89t; /A. Pronin 100b.
The Bridgeman Art Library: 120t; /© Birmingham Museums and Art Gallery 56b; / Private Collection/© Whitford & Hughes, London 97b; /Vatican Museums and Galleries, Vatican City 99br; /Museo Archeologico Nazionale, Naples 102b; /British Museum, London 110b.
Corbis: /© W. Kaehler 5.3, 54–5; © Araldo de Luca 88b.
Photo12.com: 33tr; /Oronoz 5.6, 68b, 74t, 82tr, 83bl, 94bl, 96b, 102t, 108tr, 116–17, 118t and b, 122t, 123t and b; /Ann Ronan Picture Library 119br, 120b; /ARJ 17br, 63b, 81tr and bl, 103b; /JTB Photo 35t, 121t; /Albert Arnaud 45b, 67b; /Société Française de Photographie 69b.
Werner Forman Archive: 50t; /British Museum, London 92b.

p. 1: The Theseion, Athens. p. 2: The Erechtheum, Athens. p. 3: The Laocoön. Left: Relief sculpture of horse racing.

CONTENTS

INTRODUCTION

Mention 'ancient Greece' and many people will think of temples consisting solely of columns, of blank-eyed white statues of naked men or women without arms. Such 'pure' but boring images are misleading. The temples we see today laid open to the sky are only the sunbleached skeletons of structures once adorned with statues and painted deep crimson, blue and gold. The white marble statues that today seem so chilling are seldom Greek originals (these were usually of bronze and always vividly painted) but dull, semi-competent Roman copies. The art the Greeks themselves created was more intense, astonishing and original than the art now lodged in museums. But it needs a leap of the imagination to realize this, for so much has been lost.

In painting, sculpture and architecture, Greek artists' drive toward ideal form was linked to their increasing skill at realistic depiction. The statues created by Pheidias and Polyclitus in the 5th century BC are both mathematically and anatomically perfect. With them, the human nude became the template for Greek concepts of humanized divinity. Our ideas of the perfect body, along with our ideas of architectural perfection epitomized in the Parthenon, spring from the Greeks. They envisaged the entire world in humanized form, but they also believed that mathematical principles underlie the universe.

The historian Plutarch, describing the temples of the Athenian Acropolis erected 500 years before his lifetime, wrote: "They were created in a short time for all time. Each building in its fitness was even then at once age-old. But in freshness and vigour each seems even now recent and newly made." His words apply equally powerfully to sculpture and to painting.

Left: Part of the Acropolis of Athens in 1857, site of the most famous Greek temples, as seen by the Belgian artist Florent Mols before restoration.

THE GLORY OF GREECE

Below: One of two bronze statues fished from the sea off Italy, this athlete dates from c.470BC, the dawn of Greek Classicism. It quivers with lithe energy, despite having lost all its original bright paint.

The world we live in today was made by the ancient Greeks. This is no overstatement, although the Greeks had no cars, computers or aircraft and lived very simple lives. The way we perceive both our external and internal worlds springs from the way the Greeks began to think, talk and act, with unprecedented energy, 2,500 years ago. Our architecture, astronomy, technology, medicine, athletics, theatre, maths, drama – history itself – began with the Greeks. The Greek roots of these words reveal how Greeks blazed the way that the Western world has followed since. Without the Greeks, the modern world could not exist today. Insofar as the whole world today follows Western precedents, it ultimately is following the Greeks.

The Greeks did not invent everything, of course. Egyptians and Babylonians had earlier made vital discoveries in architecture and astronomy, and Greek thinking had notable gaps – the Greeks had no concept of zero, for example. But the Greeks enjoyed in their *poleis* (their city-states), a freedom to think and speak that was lacking elsewhere at the time and in most other places for long after. In their open societies they thought and talked freely, forging artistic and intellectual prototypes for millennia to come. This happened despite – or perhaps because of – their relative poverty. Even by the standards of their time, the Greeks were far from rich.

A POWER TO SURPRISE

Greek art still has the power to surprise. People who know only white marble statues of obscure gods or heroes in museum corridors understandably feel that nothing could be more dead and cold than these frigid white males.

Above: The Charioteer of Delphi, *one of the few Greek bronze statues to survive, seems almost hieratically solemn in his long robe. Dating to c.473BC, this was an offering from Hieron, ruler of Syracuse. His eyes still have their original inlay.*

This is the wrong reaction, however. What we usually see today are dull Roman copies, in stone or marble, of lost Greek originals. Those statues, often of bronze and always brilliantly painted, with eyes inlaid with bright stones and hair separately coloured, must have once seemed thrillingly, even alarmingly, alive.

The Riace bronzes are twin statues of athletes (or warriors) fished out of the sea off Italy in 1972. Preserved almost miraculously intact, they give an idea of Greek sculpture at the start of the Classical period. The athletes, made by an unknown but brilliant artist in about 470BC, quiver with muscular energy. With traces of paint still adhering to their lips, teeth and eyes, they look as if they have just stopped exercising in the gymnasium (which is another Greek word for a

Left: The Greeks spread from their cramped peninsula across the whole Mediterranean, founding independent poleis as they went. Some of the cities, such as Marseilles, Naples and Byzantium (today Istanbul), still thrive.

Greek concept). Striding confidently forward, they appear in their nakedness almost dangerously alive and glamorous, not at all like cold statues in museums.

Even less survives of Greek painting, but sketchy if vivid murals from royal tombs in Macedonia of *c.*330BC hint at what has been lost. Later Greek painting styles, often dazzlingly realistic, survive in copies made in Pompeii, buried intact by Vesuvius' eruption in AD79.

Greek temples, their architects' supreme achievement, looked very different from today's austere ruins, being painted and even gilded in ways that might strike modern eyes as shockingly gaudy. (Such decoration served to emphasize, not disguise, their form, however.) When complete, the buildings and statues on Athens' Acropolis glittered in the sunlight, trumpeting the pride – or arrogance – of the world's first democracy.

MYTHIC RESONANCES

Every culture has its myths, sometimes embodying archetypal human truths, but few legends have proved so enduringly inspirational as the Greeks'. We still talk casually of someone's Achilles heel, of Pandora's box or Herculean labours. Greek myth has also provided universal metaphors or analogies for some of the greatest modern artists and scientists.

Freud, father of psychoanalysis, kept a statue of the Sphinx – Egyptian in origin, but absorbed into Greek legend – in his study in Vienna, along with statues of Eros. Picasso, before painting *Guernica*, the 20th century's most famous painting, returned to the myth of the Minotaur. The Minotaur is one of his most compelling images because this half-human, half-taurine monster expresses perfectly the artist's anguish about war.

ATHLETES AS HEROES

Modern concepts of the perfect body derive from Greek ideals. Physical excellence was seen as part of a holistic concept of life, uniting body, mind and spirit. Victorious athletes returned home to be greeted as heroes, touched with divinity. Statues, such as the *Charioteer of Delphi* were raised to their triumphs, and sacrifices were made to them after their deaths. The suppression of the Olympic Games in AD393 symbolized the passing of ancient Greece.

Below: This entrance corridor, dating from the 4th century BC, leads to the Stadium at Olympia. This was one of the holiest of Greek shrines, where the quadrennial Olympic Games were held for almost 1,200 years from 776BC.

TIMELINE

Ancient Greek history, both cultural and political, stretches back to the early Bronze Age in the Aegean, a time about which very little is definitely known.

The history of ancient Greece, however, does not really end with the end of antiquity, whenever that is defined. (Some time between the 4th and 7th centuries AD is the general consensus). The story of ancient Greece's cultural and intellectual influence continues long after ancient Greece itself had vanished, for the idea or ideal of Greece resurfaced in the 15th century AD in Renaissance Italy and is still powerful today.

Dates and events cluster most thickly around the great central centuries, from 500 to 300BC. This was the Classical Age in Greek culture and politics, to which later generations looked back in awe and often tried to emulate.

All dates mentioned are BC (BCE) unless otherwise stated. Almost all dates before 500BC, and many dates afterwards relating to cultural events, are conjectured or approximate.

Below: The theatre in the Sanctuary of Apollo at Delphi of the 4th century BC.

Above: The Late Minoan palace at Cnossus, Crete, dating to c.1500BC.

2000–600BC

2000BC Building of first palaces in Crete.
1700BC Building of new Cretan palaces after major earthquake.
1600–1550BC Zenith of Minoan art in Crete and Aegean Islands; *Lily Prince* fresco at Cnossus; first royal grave shafts at Mycenae; murals painted in Thira.
*c.*1500BC Volcanic eruption of Thira ravages central and southern Aegean.
1400BC Destruction of Cnossus palace.
*c.*1300BC Building of Palace of Nestor at Pylos, of citadel at Tiryns and 'Treasury of Atreus' at Mycenae.
1280BC Building of Lion Gate at Mycenae.
1190BC Traditional date of Trojan War.
1100BC Final collapse of Mycenaean civilization; beginning of Dark Ages.
1050BC Dorian migrations into Greece; Ionian migration to western Asia Minor.
800BC Wooden temple to Hera on Samos; start of Middle Geometric Style.
776BC First Olympic Games (traditional).
*c.*750BC Foundation of Cumae in Italy, first Greek colony in west; Homer writes *The Iliad*.
730–710BC Homer writes *The Odyssey;* Sparta's first conquest of Messenia; beginning of hoplite fighting.
700BC Hesiod writes *Theogony* and *Works and Days;* Greek colonization of western Mediterranean intensifies.
*c.*650BC Carving of *Auxere Statuette;* creation of Lion Avenue at Delos.
*c.*630BC Birth of poet Sappho.
*c.*620BC Poet Alcaeus born; *Chigi Vase.*
620BC Dracon's Law Code in Athens.

Above: Terrace of the Lions, Delos, a sacral avenue of the 7th century BC.

600–500BC

600BC Aesop traditionally compiles *Fables;* Polymedes of Argos sculpts *Cleobus* and *Biton,* a pair of *kouroi.*
594BC Legislation of Solon in Athens.
590–580s BC Poets Sappho and Alcaeus flourish in Lesbos; Temple of Artemis in Corfu; Temple of Hera at Olympia.
585BC Thales, the 'first philosopher' of Miletus, predicts solar eclipse.
575BC Birth of poet Anacreon.
570BC Births of philosophers Pythagoras and Xenophones of Colophon.
*c.*560BC *François Vase* made by Cleitias.
550BC Achaemenid Empire of Persia founded by Cyrus the Great; Sparta forms the Peloponnesian League; temples of Zeus and Apollo at Syracuse.
546BC Cyrus conquers Lydia and begins conquest of Ionian Greeks; Pisistratus reaffirms power as *tyrannos* of Athens.
540s BC Temple of Apollo at Corinth begun; temples of Hera at Samos and Artemis at Ephesus built by Theodorus of Samos (died 540BC); Exekias makes *Dionysus in a Ship,* a glazed *kylix* (cup).
525BC Emergence of black figure vases in Athens; birth of playwright Aeschylus; Treasury of Siphnians built at Delphi.
520s BC Pisistratid tyrants start Temple of Olympian Zeus in Athens.
518BC Birth of Theban poet Pindar.
511BC Phrynicus wins prize for his first tragedy.
510BC Temple of Aphaia at Aegina.
508BC Cleisthenes' radical reforms lead to full democracy in Athens.

Above: Athenian Treasury, Delphi, built by the new democracy in 510BC.

Above: The Temple to Poseidon at Sunium built c.440BC.

Above: Caryatids of the Erechtheum on the Acropolis, Athens, 4th century BC.

500–460BC

*c.*500BC Birth of Anaxagoras and Hippodamnus; Heraclitus active.

499BC Outbreak of Ionian Revolt; Athens sends force to help.

496BC Birth of Sophocles.

495BC Birth of Pericles.

494BC Defeat of Ionians by Persia; Phrynicus' play *Fall of Miletus* causes uproar in Athens.

490BC Athenians defeat Persians at Marathon; birth of Pheidias; *Apollo of Piombino* bronze nude cast.

484BC Birth of Euripides.

480BC Battles of Thermopylae and Salamis, Persian fleet destroyed; *Critios Boy* made: first truly classical statue.

479BC Persian army defeated at Battle of Plataea.

477BC Critios and Nesiotes sculpt (2nd) statues of Harmodius and Aristogeiton.

473BC *Charioteer of Delphi* bronze.

472BC Aeschylus's *Persians* staged.

471BC Ostracism of Themistocles.

*c.*470BC Birth of Socrates; death of Phrynicus; Riace bronzes made.

*c.*468BC *Labours of Hercules* frieze carved by 'Master of Olympia'.

467BC Battle of Eurymedon – end of Persian threat to Aegean.

462BC Democratic reforms of Ephialtes and Pericles.

*c.*460BC Outbreak of war between Sparta and Athens; birth of Hippocrates, first great physician; bronze *Zeus* from Sunium cast; *Amazonomachia Vase* made by 'Niobe Master'.

460–430BC

458BC Pericles completes reforms; Aeschylus' *Oresteia*; Long Walls of Athens.

457BC Birth of Thucydides the historian.

456BC Death of Aeschylus; completion of Temple of Zeus at Olympia.

*c.*450BC Birth of Aristophanes; Pheidias completes his first statue of Athena Lemnia; *Apollo* carved for Temple of Zeus at Olympia.

449BC Peace of Callias with Persia; Athens invites Greeks to help her restore her temples.

447BC Parthenon and the Panathenaic frieze (*Elgin Marbles*) begun.

446BC Pindar writes last *Ode*; 30 Years' Peace with Sparta (actually to 431).

443BC Ostracism of Thucydides, son of Melesias, confirms Pericles' supremacy.

440s BC Temples to Hephaestus in Athens and to Poseidon at Sunium.

438BC Gold and ivory giant statue of Athena by Pheidias set up in completed Parthenon; Euripides' *Alcestis* staged; death of Pindar.

437–432BC Propylaea built on Acropolis; Herodotus completes his *History*.

*c.*435BC *Doryphorus* (Spear-carrier) statue by Polyclitus; Anaxagoras and Protagoras teaching in Athens in Pericles' circle.

431BC Outbreak of Peloponnesian War; Pericles' Funeral Oration; Euripides' *Medea*; Pheidias creates gold and ivory statue of Zeus at Olympia.

430BC Plague devastates Athens; Pericles tried and fined; birth of Xenophon; death of Anaxagoras.

429–404BC

*c.*429BC Birth of Plato; Zeuxis, 'master of realism', painting in Athens.

428–425BC Mnesicles builds temple to Athena Nike on Acropolis; Aristophanes' *Acharnanians*; death of Herodotus.

424BC Loss of Amphipolis to Spartans leads to banishment of Thucydides, who starts writing his history of the war.

421BC Peace of Nicias; Paionius sculpts marble *Nike* in Olympia.

415BC Syracusan expedition sails under Nicias and Alcibiades; Alcibiades recalled.

413BC Disastrous loss of Syracusan expedition; Euripides' *Electra*; building of Temple of Apollo at Bassae.

411BC Oligarchic revolution at Athens.

406BC Euripides' *Bacchae* staged in Macedonia; deaths of Euripides and Sophocles.

405BC Athens' defeat at Aegospotamoi.

404BC Surrender of Athens; Long Walls pulled down; dictatorship of The Thirty.

Below: The Parthenon at Athens, the supreme Greek temple, 5th century BC.

Above: Sculpture depicting horse racing, from the Agora, Athens.

Above: Corcyra (Corfu) was one of the most important Corinthian colonies.

Above: Pillars of the Temple of Apollo, Corinth from the 6th century BC.

404–360BC

403BC Restoration of Athenian democracy and general amnesty.

401BC 'March of the 10,000' Greek mercenaries; Xenophon leads them home.

401BC Posthumous production of Sophocles' *Oedipus at Colonnus*.

400BC Death of Thucydides.

399BC Trial and execution of Socrates.

394BC Tombstone of Dexileus at Athens.

393BC Athens completes rebuilding of her Long Walls.

392BC Aristophanes' last play, *Women in Parliament*.

387BC Plato founds his Academy just outside Athens.

386BC The King's Peace: Sparta abandons Ionians in return for Persian support.

384BC Birth of Aristotle; Timotheus builds Temple of Asclepius at Epidaurus.

379BC Anti-Spartan revolution in Thebes led by Epamonindas and Pelopidas.

376BC Athens defeats Spartan fleet at Naxos; Mausolus becomes satrap of Caria; Jason establishes rule in Pherae.

375BC Praxiteles carves *Satyr Pouring Wine* for Athenian Agora.

371BC Peace of Callias between Sparta and Athens; Thebes defeats Spartans at Leuctra, becoming hegemon.

369BC Foundation of Messene and liberation of *helots* by Thebans.

367BC Dionysius I of Syracuse dies, succeeded by Dionysius II; Plato visits Syracuse to teach Dionysius philosophy.

362BC Epamonindas' death at Mantinea ends Thebes' hegemony.

360–330BC

359BC Accession of Philip II of Macedon.

357BC Philip marries Olympias.

356BC Birth of Alexander the Great.

352BC Philip defeats Phocians and becomes *tagus* (ruler) of Thessaly.

350BC Praxiteles sculpts *Aphrodite of Cnidus*; Scopas sculpting Maenads.

354BC Demosthenes' first public speech; murder of Dion in Syracuse.

347BC Death of Plato; Aristotle leaves Athens; building of Mausoleum at Halicarnassus with sculptures by Scopas.

341BC Birth of Epicurus in Samos.

340BC Philip attacks Byzantium; Alexander left as regent of Macedonia; Lysippus sculpts *Apoxymenos*.

338BC Battle of Chaeronaea: Theban and Athenian armies defeated by Philip.

337BC Council of Corinth elects Philip as general to lead anti-Persian crusade.

336BC Philip II murdered; accession of Alexander III.

335BC Alexander destroys Thebes; Aristotle starts teaching at Athens, founds Lyceum; Apelles painting at court of Alexander.

334BC Alexander crosses to Asia; defeats Persians at Granicus; liberates Ionia.

333BC Alexander routs Persians at Issus.

331BC Foundation of Alexandria; trip to consult oracle at Siwah; Alexander routs Persians at Gaugamela; enters Babylon.

330BC Praxiteles carves *Hermes and the Infant Dionysus*; *Abduction of Persephone* murals painted at royal tombs, Vergina; Apelles paints *Battle of Issus* mural.

329–300BC

326BC Alexander reaches northern India, where his troops force him to turn back.

323BC Alexander dies in Babylon; Lamian War, revolt of Greeks against Macedonia.

322BC Ptolemy gains control of Egypt: Greeks defeated by Macedonia; deaths of Demosthenes and Aristotle; Athenian democracy curbed.

***c*.320BC** Ptolemy Leochares sculpts *Apollo Belvedere*; Lysippus sculpts *Hermes*; *Deer Hunt* mosaic from Pella by Gnosis.

317BC Menander's comedy *Dyscolus*.

312BC Seleucus I takes over eastern satrapies; founds Seleucia-on-the-Tigris.

310BC Birth of poet Theocritus and astronomer Aristarchus.

307BC Epicurus settles in Athens and begins teaching philosophy.

***c*.300BC** Zeno of Citium founds Stoic School in Athens.

301BC Battle of Ipsus: division of Hellenistic world into 4 main kingdoms.

Below: The Theseion, Athens, 5th century BC, one of the city's best preserved temples.

Above: Greece's mountainous nature meant the country was relatively poor.

Above: The Cycladic island of Delos was sacred to the god Apollo.

Above: Olympia was the site of Greece's greatest athletic festival.

299–200BC

295BC Ptolemy I founds Library at Alexandria; Euclid starts writing his mathematical *Elements*.
287BC Birth of Archimedes in Syracuse.
281BC Seleucus I defeats and kills Lysimachus, then is murdered himself; Antiochus I succeeds him (to 261).
279BC Building of Pharos at Alexandria.
***c.*275BC** Aristarchus of Samos proposes heliocentric theory.
274–232BC Reign of Asoka, first Buddhist emperor in India, of part Greek descent.
270BC Hieron emerges as saviour of Syracuse, assuming crown as Hieron II.
264BC First Punic War between Carthage and Rome starts.
***c.*255BC** Bactria breaks away from Seleucid control, its example followed by Parthia.
250BC *Nike* of Samothrace sculpted.
229BC Athens 'buys out' Macedonian garrison, in effect becoming neutral.
c.225BC Eratosthenes calculates circumference of the Earth.
221BC Philip V succeeds to Macedonian throne (to 179BC); Ptolemy IV defeats Antiochus III at Raphia (218).
218–201BC Second Punic War.
217BC Peace Conference at Naupactus: warning of the 'shadow of Rome'.
216BC Battle of Cannae.
212BC Fall of Syracuse to Romans: Archimedes killed in the fighting.
202BC Hannibal finally defeated at Zama.
200BC Egypt, defeated by Antiochus III at Ionion, loses southern Syria/Palestine.
200BC *Boy Pulling Thorn from Foot* sculpted.

199–1BC

197BC Rome defeats Macedonia at Cynoscephalae in 2nd Macedonian War.
190BC *The Finding of Telephus* mural painted at Pergamum.
188BC Treaty of Apamea: Seleucids, defeated by Rome, lose Asia Minor.
180–160BC Pergamum Altar erected.
168BC Polybius taken to Rome as hostage.
166BC Romans enslave 150,000 Epirotes, make Delos a free port; slave trade booms.
***c.*150BC** Demetrius of Alexandria paints *topographoi* landscapes; First Pompeiian Style of wall painting emerges.
146BC Romans sack Corinth; make Achaea and Macedonia Roman provinces.
120BC Nile Mosaic from Praeneste.
***c.*100BC** Hagesandros sculpts *Venus de Milo*; *Alexander Mosaic* made at Pompeii.
86–85BC Sulla sacks Athens.
***c.*80BC** Second Pompeiian Style.
78BC Cicero studies at the Academy.
66–63BC Pompey reorganizes the east.
50BC *Laocoön* copy made in Rhodes.
***c.*45BC** Cicero writes *Scipio's Dream*.
44BC Caesar assassinated; renewed Roman civil wars.
44–22BC Strabo the geographer active.
42BC Battle of Philippi: Cassius and Brutus defeated by Antony and Octavian; Antony takes eastern empire, winters in Athens.
31BC Battle of Actium: Cleopatra and Antony defeated by Octavian.
30BC Egypt annexed to Roman Empire.
4BC Birth of Seneca, philosopher, and Apollonius of Tyana, mystic; Third Pompeiian Style of wall painting emerges.

AD1–1462

AD14 Augustus, first emperor of Rome, dies.
AD46 Birth of Plutarch, historian.
AD60s Heron active in Alexandria.
AD65 Death of Seneca.
AD87 Birth of Arrian, historian/general.
AD120 Birth of Pausanias, travel writer; building starts on Hadrian's Villa at Tivoli.
AD131 Hadrian completes Temple of Zeus in Athens, becomes *archon* (ruler).
AD140s Ptolemy, astronomer/cartographer, active in Alexandria.
AD160s Galen, physician, active in Rome.
AD169 Emperor Marcus Aurelius starts writing philosophical *Meditations*.
AD204 Birth of Plotinus in Alexandria.
AD250s/60s Plotinus teaching in Rome, Emperor Gallienus among his students.
AD313 Edict of Milan: Emperor Constantine I accepts Christianity.
AD324–30 Constantinople founded as 'New Rome'.
AD361–3 Emperor Julian's *Orations and Letters Against the Christians*.
AD393 Last Olympic Games held.
AD395 Roman Empire finally divided.
AD410 Sack of Rome by Goths.
AD412 St Augustine begins writing *The City of God*.
AD485 Death of Neoplatonist Proclus.
AD529 Justinian I closes Academy and other philosophy schools in Athens.
1438 Gemiston Plethon unveils esoteric Neoplatonism in Italy.
1453 Fall of Constantinople to Turks.
1462 New Platonist Academy founded in Renaissance Florence.

CHAPTER I

THE RISE OF GREEK ARCHITECTURE

Greek architecture, at its zenith in 480–320BC, did not have a long history. The Minoans and Mycenaeans had raised sophisticated buildings, but these were forgotten in the Dark Ages after 1200BC. When the Greeks began building again after 700BC, they started from scratch. Within 300 years they moved from timber and mud-brick huts to the symmetrical all-marble Parthenon in Athens. This meteoric rise owed a little to external influences but it soon became an original, self-sustaining achievement. If, after 400BC, Greek architecture changed only slowly, this did not bother the Greeks. They were less interested in ephemeral fashion than in perfection. This explains why they long stuck to *trabeated* architecture, dependent on column and lintel, although they knew of *arcuated* architecture, which involved the use of arches, vaults and domes.

A Greek temple was intended to be viewed from the outside. Today we see Greek temples almost inside out, with their interiors open to the sky, their exteriors stripped of all colouring and adornment. The Greeks never believed decoration was a crime, although they painted buildings to emphasize the forms, not disguise them. The forms themselves were perfection. Greeks also built *stoas* (porticoes), theatres, council halls and fountains.

Left: All Greek temples were brightly decorated. Only marble skeletons remain, their inner sanctuaries now open to the sky.

MINOAN ARCHITECTURE
2000–1400BC

Above: The Grand Staircase of the Palace at Cnossus, with its tapering Minoan columns, dates from c.1550BC.

Below: The Palace at Cnossus was laid out around courts, passages and staircases in a seemingly haphazard way – perhaps the origin of the myth of the Labyrinth.

The first European architecture emerged in Minoan Crete in *c.*2000BC. Minoan culture (named after the mythical King Minos) spread across the Aegean, but its centre was Crete. The Minoans' origins remain uncertain, but they were almost certainly not Greeks. Their buildings, while colourful, comfortable and ingenious, lack the Greeks' passion for symmetry. But the Minoans deeply influenced the Mycenaeans, who *were* Greek.

Cretan architecture focused on palaces, not tombs, temples or citadels. The Minoans built palaces not on a superhuman scale to overawe their subjects, as in Egypt or Babylonia, but as cheerfully decorated rambling homes and administrative centres. All had large storerooms with jars containing olive oil and wine. They were also unfortified. This suggests an unusually peaceful culture, possibly relying on a navy for external defence. (Traditionally, Minos was the first ruler of the seas.) Cnossus and Phaestus are the largest, best-excavated palace sites, but there were several other smaller sites, some termed 'royal villas'.

THE FIRST PALACES

The first palaces arose around 2000BC as increased trading links with Asia and Egypt quickened economic life. Asian and Egyptian models may have first inspired Minoan builders but they soon developed distinctive features. These include light-wells, alabaster veneer over walls made of mud-brick, ashlar or gypsum, columns made of inverted tree trunks tapering downwards, and porched courts. Often fine staircases lead to the *piano nobile* (main floor) with the best rooms upstairs, anticipating a later Mediterranean custom.

The most striking feature of the first palaces is the absence of any real plan. Rooms and courtyards seem to have been added piecemeal as need arose. The perhaps deliberate asymmetry has led to Minoan architecture being called 'accumulative'. The overall effect is pleasingly picturesque rather than grandly imposing.

CNOSSUS: HOUSE OF THE DOUBLE AXE

Around 1700BC a devastating earthquake destroyed most major buildings in Crete – the island is notoriously seismic – and all the palaces were rebuilt. This time there are signs of planning at least at Cnossus, the greatest palace, which was colourfully, if controversially, half-restored by the archaeologist Arthur Evans in the early 20th century. He thought that Cnossus now ruled the whole island.

At Cnossus a grand central court 91.5m (nearly 100 yards) long formed the new palace's core. Aligned nearly north–south, the court was flanked by colonnaded terraces rising three, perhaps four floors above. Opening off it to the west lay the Throne Room, the throne flanked by superb griffin frescoes. To the east rose a Grand Staircase, now reconstructed,

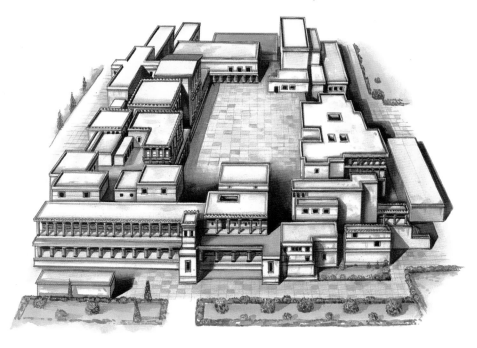

while beneath was the 'Queen's Megaron', decorated with gay frescoes of dolphins. Nearby was a bathroom with running water and flushing toilet, more advanced than anything known much later in classical Greece.

A suite of rooms nearby, the finest on the ground floor, is called the Hall of the Double Axes from the two-bladed axes, religious symbols, carved on its walls. It also served as a throne room. The Hall was open at both ends, with columns separating it from a light well at the west. Beyond a colonnade was another light well. There were no solid internal walls, only wooden partitions fitted with double doors. Open in summer and closed in winter, these kept the apartments comfortable all year. There were similar rooms on the floor above.

West of the courtyard ran a maze of magazines holding vases of oil, connected by dark corridors. These probably inspired the legend of the Labyrinth in which lurked the Minotaur, bull-headed offspring of Queen Pasiphae and a bull, eating Athenian maidens. But the overall

Below: A reconstruction of the Throne Room at Cnossus, where King Minos may once have sat, flanked by painted griffins.

tone of the palace is cheerful. It should really be called the House of the Double Axe, *labrys* meaning 'axe' in Lydian, a language related to old Cretan. Covering 2ha (5 acres), Cnossus was the largest, most sophisticated building in the Mediterranean world. Phaestus and other smaller palaces echoed its splendours, all being brightly painted inside and out, with tapering dark red or blue pillars rising above landscaped gardens. All were destroyed between 1500 and 1400BC.

Above: Phaestus in southern Crete was the site of the second-largest palace, similar in overall design to Cnossus.

Below: Minoan palaces rose to four or even five floors, with light wells flanked by columns.

MYCENAE: A CITADEL-PALACE
1550–1100BC

Above: The Mycenaeans were brilliant engineers, building huge corbelled domes of great sophistication.

Below: The Lion Gate, the monumental entrance to Mycenae, built c.1280BC.

Mycenaean buildings were very different from the Minoans'. The Mycenaeans – whom Homer called Achaeans – had overrun the peninsula by 1900BC. A war-like Greek-speaking people, they came into contact with the Minoans around 1600BC, growing wealthy through trading, raiding or fighting as mercenaries. After 1450BC they dominated Crete itself, trading from Sicily to Egypt. They used their wealth to transform their hill forts into elaborate citadels. Inside them the Achaean warrior-kings built palaces that reveal their debt to Minoan culture.

MYCENAE "RICH IN GOLD"

Greatest of their citadel-palaces was Mycenae, "rich in gold" in Homer's words. Mycenae dominated the fertile Argolid plain, controlling the trade routes to the Corinthian Isthmus. In legend, its rulers, the feuding Atreids, were acknowledged as High Kings by other Greeks. Its lords and those of nearby Tiryns have left the most dramatic fortifications in Bronze Age Europe before the Middle Ages.

At the centre of every Mycenaean palace and large house lay a *megaron* (great hall). Square or rectangular, this room had four pillars around an open circular hearth, often under a lantern roof that let smoke out and light in. The megaron served as the main baronial hall and sometimes as the throne room. (At Mycenae there was another throne room.) A *propylaeum* (ceremonial gateway) was common at the megaron's entrance, often with a porched court in front of that.

All were arranged on a clear axis to create an imposing approach. The axial plan of Mycenaean buildings resurfaced in later Greek architecture. Beyond or above the megaron lay private royal apartments, built of timber and mud-brick like most Mycenaean dwellings. These had murals so Minoan in style that Cretan artists might have been employed, but the themes – horses, chariots, warriors – were very different from Crete. Bathrooms similar to those at Cnossus have been found at Tiryns and elsewhere, but much of Mycenae's royal palace has fallen down a ravine.

THE LION GATE

A visitor to Mycenae at its 13th-century peak would have approached up a steep well-paved chariot road to see the Lion Gate towering above him. Built c.1280BC, it was part of massive fortifications enclosing the whole hill. The Lion Gate consists of three giant slabs of cut ashlar, with the lintel surmounted by two great stone-carved lions, whose now-lost heads once turned to snarl downward. The regal menace of this sculpture derives from Hittite models (in Anatolia), but the lions flank a Minoan-style column, revealing a cultural mixture. Entering, the visitor would pass on the right tomb circles from the 16th century BC (where the archaeologist Heinrich Schliemann later found

what he thought was the mask of Agamemnon.) A chariot ramp zigzagged up to the palace, but those on foot could use a direct staircase.

While the palace itself was small compared to that at Cnossus, let alone those in Egypt – its court measured only 15 by 9m (50 by 30ft) and the megaron was about the same size – it was flanked by sizeable other houses such as the House of Columns. A smaller version of the palace, its colonnaded court anticipates those of wealthy Greek dwellings 1,000 years later. There were no great temples, the Mycenaeans presumably conducting their worship outside.

'TREASURY OF ATREUS'

The most imposing Mycenaean structure is a tomb, the 'Treasury of Atreus', so-called because of a misconception by its discoverers. Lying outside the citadel and dating from *c.*1280BC, it might have been the tomb of Agamemnon, the Achaean leader in the Trojan Wars, and others of the Atreid dynasty. It is a *tholos*, a circular chamber with a dome made of corbelled stone resembling a beehive. It is entered by a 38m (120ft) long *dromos*, a long narrow passageway burrowing into the earth, with walls of cut stone giving a suitably sepulchral approach. The door to the tomb has tapering sides and an inward slant, a style derived from Egypt. Above it is a triangular opening to relieve pressure on the lintel, once richly decorated with Minoan-style spirals.

The tomb's doors, originally of bronze, were flanked by columns of green limestone crowned with mouldings resembling Egyptian water-lily capitals. The tholos chamber, 13m (43ft) high and 14.5m (47ft 6in) in diameter, had a smooth interior surface once covered with gold, silver and bronze decorations. Although a tholos is not a 'true' dome – a corbelled dome relies on corbelled or projecting stones to close the gap – the 'Treasury of Atreus' remained the world's largest masonry dome until the building of the Pantheon in Rome 1,400 years later.

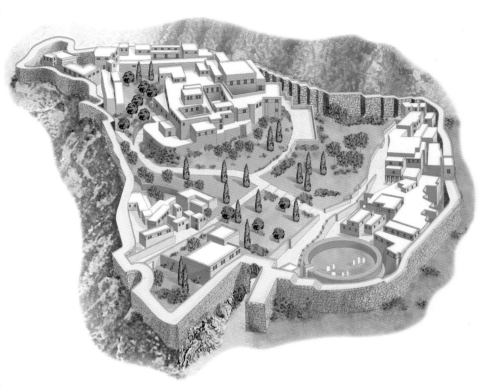

Above: A reconstruction of the citadel at Mycenae protected by its massive walls, for long the greatest in all Greece.

Below: The so-called 'Treasury of Atreus' at Mycenae, actually a vast royal tholos-type tomb, where the kings of Mycenae were buried in splendour with their treasures.

TIRYNS AND PYLOS
CONTRASTING PALACES 1500–1150 BC

Above: A passage within the massive Cyclopean walls of Tiryns, the most complete Mycenaean citadel-palace to have survived.

Below: The megalithic walls at Tiryns, still standing after 3,200 years, which later Greeks thought must be the work of giants.

Two very different palaces in the Peloponnese's far corners reveal the variety of Mycenaean palace architecture.

TIRYNS: THE MIGHTY CITADEL

Tiryns, standing on a ridge a few miles to the south-east, is better preserved than Mycenae, though lacking its dramatic legendary associations. Homer called it "mighty-walled". This is, most unusually for Homer, a poetic understatement, for its walls are truly massive, being 6m (20ft) thick and originally even higher.

The upper citadel was fortified in c.1400BC along the crest of the ridge. Its walls were formed of massive rough-hewn blocks, probably inspired by Hittite examples in Anatolia. (The Mycenaeans and Hittites were in diplomatic and trading contact, so knowledge of the massively fortified Hittite citadel at Hattusa could have reached Greece.) The main Eastern Gate at first opened directly on to the slope but was progressively improved until the gate was approached from the north and then along a passageway between high walls.

Huge walls, in places 10m (33ft) thick and at least as high, lined this. Galleries in the walls' thickness had embrasures through which defenders could shoot arrows down on to any assailants. A lesser entrance was made on the west side by building out a huge tower with a doorway through it. Along the front of this protruding bastion a pit was dug and a drawbridge installed.

The palace these walls tightly enclosed was, in contrast, very modestly sized. In the 13th century BC it was reconstructed with a Minoan-style outer propylaeum, which measured approximately 13.5 by 13.75m (44 by 46ft) giving on to a smaller propylaeum. Beyond lay the megaron, its plastered floor painted with squares of marine life. Its design perpetuated

Minoan fashions of centuries before. So did the murals of women dressed in fashions seemingly copied from Cnossus. Around the megaron clustered the living apartments, including the bathroom. This had a 20-ton block of limestone as its floor, however, a markedly non-Minoan touch.

THE PALACE OF NESTOR

Safely distant from the Argolid's battlefields in the south-western Peloponnese are the ruins of the palace called after Nestor, Homer's venerable king. According to legend, Nestor's father came from Thessaly to found a new kingdom in Messenia. Nestor later took 90 ships to fight in the Trojan Wars, forming the second largest Greek contingent. Archaeology seems to confirm legend. An early Mycenaean settlement on a hill overlooking Navarino Bay was replaced about 1300BC by a new palace. This flourished – unwalled, most remarkably for a Mycenaean – for the next 100 years.

The Palace of Nestor is the most complete Mycenaean palace excavated. The new palace was entered from a formal propylaeum through a simple porchway with a single fluted wooden column, with a guard by the door. Across an inner courtyard paved in stucco with great pillars on both sides was a modest megaron and beyond that the Great Megaron, measuring 13 by 11.2m (42 by 37ft). At its centre was a great round hearth with a lantern to let smoke out.

Against the east wall stood the throne, flanked by frescoes of lions, griffins and deer. Here it is easy to imagine that Homeric heroes such as Nestor and Telemachus might have feasted while bards sang of the Trojan War. But Homer is never a wholly reliable guide for archaeologists. Stairs led to domestic rooms above, while to the north-east lay workshops, offices and store-rooms.

The Palace of Nestor at Pylos was, like most Aegean buildings, built of ashlar stone around a timber frame with timber pillars. This made it vulnerable

to fire, and fire destroyed the palace soon after 1200BC. From clay writing tablets baked in that fire we read of preparations to repel the invaders, perhaps northern Dorian tribes. Pylos, last and most graceful of the Mycenaean palaces, was apparently the first to fall. But refugees from Pylos sailed east. Some found shelter in Athens, the 'unsacked city', others sailed on to Ionia in the eastern Aegean.

Above: The magnificently constructed tholos tomb at Pylos, perhaps the royal burial place of the Neleid dynasty mentioned by Homer.

Below: The megaron (reconstructed) of the Palace of Nestor at Pylos, the last-built and most elegant of Mycenaean palaces.

THE DARK AGES
1100–600BC

Above: The huge columns of the Temple of Amon at Karnak were a possible influence on early Greek architecture.

Below: The Temple of Hatshepsut, Egypt, was perhaps an influence on early Greek temples.

Some time after 1200BC the Mycenaean world collapsed. In its place emerged a simpler, poorer world with limited horizons and even more limited architecture. Greeks, as we can now call them (*Greek* is a Roman name, they called themselves Hellenes) forgot the reality of Mycenaean life but hazily remembered its legendary heroes. It is uncertain if Dark Age Greeks remembered actual Mycenaean architecture, although they may have been influenced by grand Egyptian temples they saw. But over the next few centuries there was to be no building in stone at all.

THE FIRST BUILDINGS
The oldest structure unearthed is at Lefkandi on Euboea island, dating from *c.*1000BC. Remarkably large – 45 x 9m (150 by *c.*30ft) – it was perhaps a cross

Above: The Hippostyle Hall at Karnak must have awed Greek traders and mercenaries with its imposing stony grandeur.

between a tomb and temple, with a stone base but mud-brick walls and thatch roof, surrounded by a colonnaded court with timber pillars. More typical are two small temples near Corinth to Hera, the wife of Zeus, considered mother of the gods. These were simple wooden thatched huts with timber porches and rounded ends. Around 800BC a temple to Hera was built on Samos. While still built of wood, it anticipates later temples in its strict rectilinear plan. It was large – 30m (100ft) long – and *peripteral*, i.e. its inner *cella* was surrounded by an external colonnade added *c.*750BC. (It was rebuilt several times over the next centuries, each time progressively more grandly.) All these buildings had pitched roofs, unlike most Bronze Age structures.

The whole tradition of Greek architecture probably originated in the carpentry techniques needed to make these timber buildings. So thought Vitruvius, the influential Roman architect writing in the 1st century BC. In the *entablature* of the Doric

order, the first of the three Greek orders of columns (usually demonstrated in the capitals of the columns), *triglyphs* represent the end of the original wooden crossbeams, *guttae* were the pegs used to fasten them and *metopes* were the spaces between the beams. The Greeks stuck faithfully to these forms, often called 'petrified carpentry', long after they began building in stone.

CLAY TILES, STONE COLUMNS

A key development was the invention of terracotta (fired clay) roof tiles after 700BC. Tiles, being much heavier than timber or thatch – some early examples from the mid-7th century weigh 30kg (66lb) each – led to the need for stone columns and masonry walls to support them. They also produced ridge roofs with a shallower pitch. Among the first stone temples, that of Poseidon, on the Corinthian Isthmus of c.650BC, had walls wholly of cut stone, but its columns were wooden. At the Temple of Apollo at Thermon in north-western Greece of c.630BC, the upper walls were made of mud-brick but its wooden entablature (the superstructure between the capitals

and gutter) had brightly painted terracotta panels showing gorgons and other mythical creatures. Parts of this survive. Its tiled roof was supported by 15 wooden columns on each side and five at each end, a prototypical Doric temple.

By 600BC the Greeks were starting to build temples wholly in stone, with roofs made of terracotta tiles on wooden beams. By then the basic form for later Greek temples was established. Temples, flanked by columns, generally faced east, with their main altars outside. The *procella*, or vestibule, of the east front led directly to the cella, which held the statue of the god or goddess in sacred darkness.

Above: The Temple of Poseidon at Isthmia, dating from c.650BC, was one of the first Greek temples with stone walls. This picture shows it at a much later date when it was far more ornate.

Below: The Beach of Aphrodite in Cyprus, the one part of the Greek world where Mycenaean customs long survived almost unchanged.

THE EMERGENCE OF THE GREEK TEMPLE 600–530BC

Above: The Temple of Hera at Samos of c.580BC, whose lower walls still stand, is among the earliest surviving Greek temples. (The columns are of a later date.)

Below: At Selinus (Selinunte) in Sicily, three temples from the 6th century BC remain, with some massive Doric columns intact.

In the 6th century BC the tempo of Greek life began to accelerate. This cultural and social quickening reflected the economic recovery that made even archaic Greece wealthier than the Mycenaean world. Wealth was now more equally spread, also. This affected Greek architecture, for money was spent building temples for all the city, not palaces just for kings. A surge of confidence in building techniques led to the construction of early stone temples.

These temples are large, often with crudely massive Doric columns. The columns' gigantic size may reflect early architects' anxiety about supporting the new tiled roofs and masonry entablatures. Equally possibly, they were built so heavily just to impress.

From the start, all temples were designed to be seen mainly from the outside, as were almost all Greek buildings. At first, columns were overwhelmingly of the Doric order, or type. This consisted of a fluted (grooved) column rising directly from the ground like a tree trunk – early columns were often monoliths –

with a shallow capital supporting an entablature decorated with a triglyph and metope frieze. ('Doric' refers also to one of the two main Greek dialects, the other being Ionian. The Peloponnese, southern Aegean islands and many Sicilian cities were Dorian, but the Doric order was at first the architectural norm even among Ionians. The most perfect Doric temple of all is the Parthenon in Ionian Athens.)

Among the earliest temples with a full Doric order was the Temple of Artemis at Corcyra (Corfu), built *c.*590BC. Long since demolished, its pediment had sculpted figures – a giant gorgon surrounded by panthers at the front to frighten away evil spirits, with a *gigantomachia* (battle of gods and giants) on the sides. Built *c.*580BC, the Temple of Hera at Olympia, site of the Olympic Games, has its base walls still standing, although the present three Doric columns are later. Its cella walls were of limestone masonry at the base but the rest of the structure was still mud-brick.

The Temple of Apollo at Corinth from *c.*540BC has seven giant Doric columns standing. Originally there were six columns at the temple's ends and 15 on each side, each column being a limestone monolith 6.6m (21ft) high covered in stucco. Their bare forms, high above the Gulf Corinth, are still powerfully dramatic. The base under the columns rises in a gentle convex curve, the first example of *entasis*, the device to correct the illusion (if seen from a distance) of drooping in the middle that would arise if the base was really level.

TRIGLYPHS AND METOPES
This temple also shows Greek architects grappling successfully with a fundamental problem of the Doric order: Greek architects insisted on putting a triglyph over each column,

Above: The Temple of Apollo at Corinth dates from c.540BC, where seven giant Doric columns are still standing. The other 35 have long since fallen.

symbolizing the weight carried by the column. But they also wanted to end every frieze with a triglyph, not a less-powerful metope. As corner triglyphs could not be placed centrally over corner columns, end columns were placed closer together than the rest, while end metopes are 5cm (2in) wider than the others. Greek architects soon recognized such subtleties.

FIRST TEMPLES IN THE WEST

Founded in 735BC, Syracuse became one of the richest cities in this booming new world. Two Doric temples were built in Syracuse in the mid-6th century BC: the Temple of Olympian Zeus and that of Apollo. Both had 17 columns on each side and six across the end. In the Temple of Apollo, several survive and have been reinstated. They are monoliths, 8m (26ft) high, tapered and irregular in size. Those at the opposite corners of each end differ by as much as 30cm (1ft) in diameter from those at the other. The height of some columns is only four times their diameter. The effect, bulky rather than accomplished, suggests that this was a

pioneer building. At Selinus, in western Sicily, ruins remain of three huge temples, partly restored, dating also from the 6th century BC. All boast massive columns.

On the Italian mainland at Poseidonia (Paestum), the 'Basilica', actually a temple to Hera of the 6th century, has similar monumental columns with vast capitals. The bare virile power of these early temples much impressed visiting Neoclassical architects in the 18th century, who did not realize that originally all temple columns had been stuccoed.

Above: At the Temple of Apollo at Syracuse, built in the 6th century BC, monolithic Doric columns survive, exuding primitive strength.

Below: At Poseidonia (Paestum) in southern Italy, the 'Basilica', actually a temple to Hera of the 6th century BC, has monumental columns with vast overhanging capitals.

THE DEVELOPMENT OF THE GREEK TEMPLE 530–480BC

Under the Pisistratids, a dynasty of enlightened tyrants who ruled Athens intermittently from 560 to 510BC, the city became increasingly prosperous. It also emerged as one of Greece's leading cultural centres, and now began building proper Doric temples.

The Temple of Athena Polias, the divine guardian of Athens, was probably the very first temple erected on the Acropolis, being built in about 530BC. It had sculptures on its pediments carved in marble and in the round – a double first. Later, a huge temple to Olympian Zeus was started east of the Acropolis but the Pisistratids lost power in 510BC before it had progressed beyond its base plan. (It was finally completed under the Emperor Hadrian in AD130.)

After Athens' triumphant defeat of the Persians at the battle of Marathon in 490BC, a new temple to the city's goddess was started on the Acropolis and a propy-laeum built at the Acropolis entrance with fine Doric columns.

However, all the Acropolis' buildings were torched in the two Persian invasions and sacks of 480–479BC, and any reconstructions

Above: The upper colonnade of the Temple of Aphaea, c.500BC, which is most unusually part-intact.

remain predominately conjectural. While walls and columns were now of stone, roofs still had wooden beams.

THE TEMPLE OF APHAEA

The great Doric Temple of Aphaea, goddess of sailors and hunters on the island of Aegina south of Athens, survives remarkably well. Built c.510–490BC, the temple is sited on a rocky hilltop with superb views. Most of its columns survive almost up to roof level, allowing the upper colonnade to be seen half-extant for once. The *pteron* had six monolithic columns on the ends and 12 on the sides, sloping inwards to increase the impression of strength. The columns again have entasis (convex swelling) to make the columns appear regular when seen from afar. The *stylobate* has an upward curve.

Built of local limestone, the Temple of Aphaea now gleams serenely pale gold, but originally it was faced with cream-painted marble stucco and had bright-painted ornamental features such as lions' heads. Its triglyphs and guttae were painted dark blue, while other parts of the entablature were deep red – colours that were later used on the Athenian Parthenon. This again reveals how mistaken earlier ideas about Greek 'pure white marble form' were. Greek temples, like the lives of the Greek themselves, blazed with impassioned colour. The older sculptures from the temple's west pediment depict graceful smiling warriors, while figures on the east front, carved 20 years later, are more heroically muscular, indicating the revolution that was starting to transform Greek sculpture.

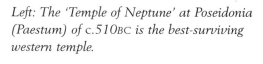

Left: The 'Temple of Neptune' at Poseidonia (Paestum) of c.510BC is the best-surviving western temple.

GIANT TEMPLES OF THE WEST

Out in the Greek west, temples were built of remarkable size, splendour and quirkiness. Most notable of these is the Temple of Olympian Zeus at Acragas (Agrigento) in south-western Sicily. Although only founded in 580BC, Acragas was among the wealthiest cities in the Greek world. It built the largest Doric temple ever, measuring 110 by 53m (361 by 173ft), with columns originally 20m (65ft) high.

The temple, started *c.*505BC, was unfinished when Carthaginians sacked the city in 406BC and almost nothing remains. Raised on a platform 4.5m (15ft) high, its huge outer columns, seven at each end and 14 along the side, were engaged (half-sunk) into the walls. This was a novel idea, perhaps designed to help carry the weight of the large entablature. At the temple's corners, however, the columns were necessarily three-quarters round. Further, the entablature, walls and half-columns were not made of solid masonry blocks but built of relatively small stones. As the diameter of each column exceeded 4m (13ft), this must have made them easier and cheaper to build.

The Acragas temple has another peculiarity, which gives it its nickname 'Temple of the Giants'. From masonry fragments since reassembled and from medieval records, made before the temple was destroyed by quarrying, we know that the temple incorporated huge male figures, about 7.6m (25ft) high, the Atlantes. (They are named after the mythical giant who upheld the heavens on his shoulders.) These titans supported the architrave, standing on a ledge, one between each pillar. Remnants of their vast forms have been tentatively reassembled. It is unlikely that the temple's interior was ever roofed over.

THE 'TEMPLE OF NEPTUNE'

North at Poseidonia (Paestum) on the Italian mainland, the so-called 'Temple of Neptune' (really yet another temple of Hera, that most important of goddesses),

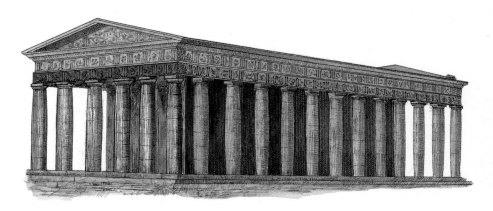

was started *c.*510BC. It has survived better than any other western temple. Its pediment, outer columns and architraves are still almost intact. It is relatively conventional in plan, with a pteron of six by 14 columns, measuring 24 by 59m (79 by 196ft). Here, too, the external columns, 8.9m (29ft) high, taper sharply, giving this temple also an impression of rugged, almost truculent strength. The western Greeks, rich but remote from the accepted conventions on the mainland, were developing an original, albeit quirky, form of architecture.

Above: A typical Doric temple showing the brightly painted and richly carved frieze and pediment, and the marble pillars, with the slight convex curve known as entasis that made them appear straight.

Below: The Temple of Aphaea on Aegina shows the Doric temple approaching perfection. It was built c.510–490BC.

THE IONIC TEMPLE
560–400BC

Above: Ionic columns are chiefly identified by their rolled-up forms resembling cushions or rams' horns, which create their distinctive volutes.

While the Doric order at first dominated the Greek world, it was soon rivalled by the Ionic order, a more slender, graceful style of column and capital (head). The Ionic order first appeared in the sophisticated Ionian cities and the Aegean islands in the 6th century BC, spreading to the mainland. It became seen as the feminine order, in contrast to the more 'virile' Doric order.

Preceding the Ionic order was the Aeolian, a capital common in Aeolis in north-western Asia Minor around 600BC. This had *volutes* (spiral scrolls) growing up and out of the column, supporting a rectangular slab. (It is now thought that there was no direct connection between the Aeolian and the Ionian orders, for the oldest Ionic capitals date only from 560BC, while their volutes, in the form of rams' horns or scrolls, turn downward and inward. Also, Aeolic columns had no bases but Ionic columns stood on elaborate bases.)

THE FIRST IONIC TEMPLES

The first true Ionic columns appeared in two vast temples: the Heraion at Samos and the Artemision at Ephesus. Remarkably similar, they were both built in the mid-6th century BC by Theodorus of Samos (died 540BC). An architect of genius, he wrote the first architectural treatise, now lost. King Croesus of Lydia, wealthy overlord of Ephesus, paid for most of its temple. Both buildings were dipteral, i.e. they had a double *pteron* (colonnade), an imposing feature perhaps inspired by Egyptian examples.

Both temples were later destroyed by fire, although that at Ephesus was rebuilt more grandly to become one of the Seven Wonders of the World in the Hellenistic and Roman ages. Both had two rows of eight columns at the entrance, with the columns' spacing and thickness gradually increasing toward the centre to make them look regular seen from afar, as with most Greek temples. At the Heraion on Samos the two central columns were 8.6m (28ft) apart while the outermost pairs were only 5.9m (17ft) apart. It was about 88.4 by 45.7m (290 by 150ft).

The Temple of Artemis at Ephesus was even larger, measuring 109 by 55m (358 by 171ft). Built of limestone covered in marble, the first temple to be so built, its tall, slender columns had richly moulded bases, each with a horizontally fluted *torus*. Sculptural display was ornamental rather than structural in a way that became typically Ionian.

Left: The Ionic columns of the north porch of the Erechtheum, started in 421BC and completed in 405BC, are among the earliest extant uses of the Ionic order in Athens.

Ionic columns had no triglyphs or metopes. Instead, in Asiatic Ionic temples rows of *dentils* ran below the cornice, while in west Aegean Ionic style there was a band of stone, often richly sculpted.

THE TREASURY OF THE SIPHNIANS

One of the first half-extant Ionic temples, built in 525BC, the Treasury of the Siphnians at Delphi, was also the first marble temple on the mainland. Although its base is limestone, its superstructure uses Siphnian marble for the main wall, Naxian for its outer decorations and Parian for its sculptural adornments. Its porch boasts two large free-standing *caryatids* (female statues) similar to those later erected at the Erechtheum on the Athenian Acropolis. The caryatids wear tall hats carved with figures of men and lions. The frieze and even the pediment have sculpted figures carved in high relief, all once brightly painted in red, blue and green. Unpainted, fresh-cut marble must have gleamed blindingly white in strong Greek sunlight.

BUILDING IN MARBLE

Although Greece was blessed with abundant limestone, Greek architects around 500BC began to realize that building completely in marble made it possible to produce far clearer, crisper outlines for both orders of columns. However, marble was very expensive except near quarries. The first major use of marble in temple-building at the Artemision of Ephesus was made possible by King Croesus, a famously rich ruler. Pisistratus reputedly used marble roof tiles for his Temple of Athena Polias in the 530s BC, but he had connections with Paros. Even for the Siphnians, it must have been costly to haul the marble for their small treasury up the mountains to Delphi.

Once they had done so, however, others felt the urge to compete. Cleisthenes, the wealthy Athenian radical aristocrat, probably sponsored the building of the Treasury of the Athenians *c.*500BC. This, also resembling a mini-temple, is the first

Doric all-marble building. In Athens itself marble remained forbiddingly expensive until a quarry was opened on nearby Mt Pentelicus soon after 500BC. When Athens finally began rebuilding after the end of the Persian wars, it found marble of the highest quality on its doorstep. New claw chisels were needed to work this harder, more brittle material, but the remarkable results on the Acropolis astound us still.

Above: The Treasury of the Athenians at Delphi built soon after 500BC, resembling a mini-temple, is the first Greek all-marble structure, and still Doric in style.

THE PARTHENON
A PERFECT TEMPLE

Above: The Parthenon, perhaps the most famous temple in the world, was built by Ictinus and Callicrates from 447BC. It brought the Doric temple to perfection.

Below: The Parthenon on the Acropolis as it may have looked in its prime, lavishly decorated and colourfully painted. Built as a gleaming statement of Athenian national pride, it housed the great cult statue of Athena, tutelary goddess of the city.

When the Athenians returned to their burnt-out city in 479BC after the Persians had been defeated, they ignored the blackened stumps of their temples on the Acropolis. In the Oath of Plataea that year they had sworn not to rebuild the temples as a reminder of Persian sacrilege in burning them. For decades anyway, they were occupied in fighting Persia. But in 449BC the Persian wars ended with the Peace of Callias. The Athenians then debated what to do with the tribute money still flowing in from their allied (or, increasingly, their subject) states in the Delian League.

Pericles – the radical aristocrat who so dominated the age that he has given his name to it – urged the money be used to rebuild the city's temples. His proposal triggered a violent debate. Some Athenians agreed with Thucydides, son of Melesias, cousin of the historian, that this would be a misuse of the funds. But Pericles won the argument.

Work began in 447BC on what many consider the world's most perfect building: the Parthenon, temple of Athena, virgin (*parthenos*) goddess of the city. Within 15 years the Parthenon had been completed. It has become the archetypal image of ancient Greece.

Above: The frieze running around the Parthenon showing horsemen in the Panathenaic Procession, carved to the general designs of Pheidias.

Pheidias, the great sculptor, had overall charge of the project, but the joint architects were Callicrates and Ictinus. The latter wrote a book about the Parthenon's construction, which, like much Greek literature, has been lost. But the temple itself embodies the key principles of Greek classicism so closely that it has been read almost like a book by successive archaeologists.

FOR THE GODS' EYES ONLY?

A strange aspect of the Parthenon is the position of the frieze, 161m (534ft) long, running high up around the cella's exterior. Meticulously carved, this must have been almost impossible for contemporary observers to see fully, being overshadowed by the architrave above when the temple was intact. The outer columns would have half-obscured it if seen from far-off. To look at the frieze standing close up on the stylobate must have required painful neck-craning. Possibly it was designed only for the all-seeing eyes of the gods. In this it anticipates Gothic cathedral carvings.

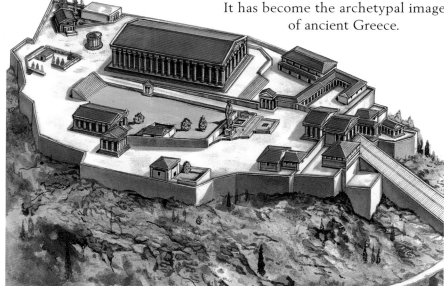

MARBLE COLUMNS AND GILDED STATUES

The building of such a huge marble structure in less than ten years – the sculpting took a further five years to complete – was an unprecedented feat. About 22,000 tons of marble were needed for the Parthenon and the Propylaea, the ceremonial gateway. Fortunately, Mt Pentelicum's quarries were only 13km (8 miles) away. Marble column drums surviving from the burnt earlier temple to Athena were incorporated into the new building, which rested partly on its predecessor's base.

The pteron measured eight by 17 columns, obeying the now canonical rule that the number of columns on the sides should be more than double those on the ends. The columns' height is 5.48 times their diameter, 10.4m (34.3ft) high. The stylobate, as usual, had three steps all round. Sited on the Acropolis' southern edge, the Parthenon remains strikingly visible from miles off. (It also remained essentially intact until its interior was wrecked in an explosion in 1683. That year the Venetians were besieging Athens, held by Turkish troops who were storing gunpowder in the temple. One direct hit gutted the Parthenon.)

In antiquity, worshippers who entered the Acropolis would at first have seen only the temple's carved pediment looming above a flanking wall. As they passed the Propylaea, their eyes would be caught by Pheidias' great outdoor bronze statue of Athena Promachos, 'the warrior', visible far out at sea. Turning a corner, worshippers could finally see the temple's east front ahead and enter the cella. Almost 30m (100ft) long by 10m (34ft) wide and divided in two, this was made of finely cut ashlar blocks. In its inner chamber stood the chryselephantine (gold-ivory over a wooden core) statue of the goddess, Pheidias' masterwork. A two-storeyed Doric colonnade framed the statue, while the outer chamber had internal Ionic columns, a radical innovation inside a Doric temple.

Unusually, all the metopes were sculpted in high relief, the pediments being filled with groups of figures, vividly painted. These include works by Pheidias depicting the city's legends. At each corner a lion's head was carved on the cornice, while above gilded winged victories mounted on *acroteria* seemed poised for flight.

TECHNICAL 'REFINEMENTS'

The Parthenon is renowned for its technical 'refinements', which make it the most accomplished of Doric temples. These include entasis and inward-tilting columns, so that those at the corners do not appear thinner, and the convexity in the stylobate and entablature. All were designed to make the temple look perfectly proportioned when seen from far off. (The columns' tilt means that theoretically they would meet in the sky 2.4km (1½ miles) above.)

Working in marble permitted such sophistication but inevitably required remarkable skills from the workforce. Their efforts produced the archetypal Greek temple.

Above: A view of the Parthenon from the north. It remained astonishingly intact until an explosion during a siege in 1683 blew it apart – it was being used to store gunpowder by the Turks.

Below: The Acropolis of Athens seen from afar, with its unsurpassable group of superb 5th-century BC temples.

ON THE ACROPOLIS
THE OTHER TEMPLES

Above: Jutting out high over the city, the tiny temple to Athena Nike, the first visible to worshippers approaching the Acropolis, was built in 428–425BC, probably by Mnesicles.

Below: The Erechtheum, completed in 405BC, rivals the Parthenon in elegance and surpasses it in ingenuity. It is named after Athens' legendary first king, Erechtheus. The close-spaced supporting caryatids emphasize the building's mass.

Around the Parthenon, smaller temples were subsequently built on the Acropolis, despite the war with the Peloponnesians that started in 431BC. Remarkably, even through the war's increasing disasters, work continued intermittently, bringing Greek classical architecture to its peak.

The Propylaea, the monumental Doric gateway at the west of the Acropolis, was the second building commissioned by Pericles. It was constructed in 437–432BC, work on it stopping before completion as war loomed. Little is known about its architect Mnesicles, but he probably also designed the Athena Nike temple opposite. The Propylaea was approached by a ramp about 25m (65ft) wide, the start of the Panathenaic Way leading down to the Agora (market place). It had two impressive temple-like façades of six Doric columns, one on each side.

IRON BARS AND CUNNING
Mnesicles solved the difficulty of erecting a symmetrical building on a sloping, irregular site by extending the architrave round the flanking buildings on the same level. However, the exterior junction of the Propylaea's separate roofs must have looked awkward. The building is entered through a hexastyle (six-column) Doric porch, the two central columns being wider spaced to let sacrificial animals pass through. Beyond lay an imposing passage with Ionic columns supporting a rich marble ceiling. This, with its coffers (recessed panels) adorned with gold stars on a blue background, was a wonder of its age. It was also very expensive, the building costing 2,000 talents. The architraves over the colonnade were reinforced with iron bars, a remarkable innovation if superfluous structurally. Designing the Propylaea, the first complex building on different levels, required creating harmonious spatial relations between its varied parts. It inspired many later architects.

On the Propylaea's north side lay the *pinakotheke* (the picture gallery), where state banquets were held with platforms for dining couches round the walls. It also housed some of Athens' greatest pictures, depicting victories over the Persians at Marathon and Salamis, all long since lost.

On the other side of the Propylaea the tiny temple to Athena Nike was built, probably by Mnesicles, in *c.*428–425BC. It uses the Ionic order with four mono-lithic columns only 4m (13ft) high at each end, oddly thick for their size. The aim was probably to avoid too strong a contrast to the solid Propylaea. It had attachments for figures in its pediments and much fine carving, while its little cella is almost square. Jutting out high over the city, this exquisite temple is the first approaching visitors see.

THE ERECHTHEUM
Another Ionic temple on the Acropolis, the Erechtheum rivals the Parthenon in elegance if not size. Started in 421BC after the short-lasting Peace of Nicias and completed in 405BC, the year of Athens'

Above: The Propylaea, the monumental Doric gateway on the west of the Acropolis, was built in 437–432BC, work stopping before its completion as war loomed. Its architect was Mnesicles.

final catastrophic defeat, it was named after the legendary semi-divine first king of Athens. It is in fact a multiple temple, housing shrines to ten different gods and heroes, besides a pit of sacred serpents. Because the site is asymmetrical and on several levels, the Erechtheum is really two semi-detached temples with three porches facing in different directions. The asymmetry is minimized by the noble exterior, united by a harmonious Ionic order and frieze of low-relief figures in white marble on a dark background running around the temple like a belt. The whole Erechtheum, again built of marble, has carvings of an elaboration never repeated elsewhere in Greece.

The central larger temple, dedicated to Athena Polias (guardian), has a huge porch facing north over the city. It housed her ancient wooden statue, dating back to the Bronze Age, besides the supposed tomb of Erechtheus. Its smaller porch, on the south side facing the Parthenon, has famous caryatids (now copies) instead of supporting pillars. These draped female figures are close-spaced to create a massiveness echoing the Parthenon's.

The south porch, lower than the north, is raised on a wall to make it appear level. It was linked internally by a staircase.

The eastern temple was dedicated chiefly to Zeus, whose altar was in the porch. Inside were altars to Hephaestus, the fire god, Erechtheus and Poseidon. At the Erechtheum's west end stood the Pandroseum, an enclosure with the tomb of Cecrops, another Athenian mythical hero, and the sacred olive tree of Athena. Reputedly it sprouted fresh leaves after being burnt by the Persians in 480BC. The Erechtheum's interior suffered from being converted into the Turkish governor's harem under Ottoman rule (1455–1829).

Above: The hill of the Acropolis, towering above Athens, superbly displays the highest achievements of Greek classical architecture.

Below: The Erechtheum was a temple not to one deity but to ten, being in reality two semi-detached buildings with three porches, all on different levels. Its architect may also have been Mnesicles.

OTHER TEMPLES OF THE GOLDEN AGE

Above: The Temple of Poseidon the sea-god at Sunium was built by an unknown architect around 440BC. Superbly sited at Sunium on the point of Attica, it is made of local marble.

Below: The Hephaistion (Theseion) on the west side of the Agora was Athens' first all-marble temple. It was started in 449BC, being designed by the same unknown architect who built that at Sunium. It has survived better than any other Greek temple.

Although the temples on the Acropolis are Athens' most striking, many others were built in the city and across Greece in the 5th century BC. Oldest of the classical temples in central Athens itself was the Hephaistion (once called the Theseion) on the west of the Agora, the city's social and commercial heart.

Started in 449BC, it is the first all-marble Doric temple in Attica but lacks the Parthenon's subtleties. Its use of 'refinements' such as entasis is crudely obvious, so that the building only convinces when seen front-on. Happily, that is how most Athenians would have seen it, as trees or buildings on its sides probably prevented other views. Further, all its sculptured metopes are concentrated on its front or just around its corners. The relatively high entablature of 2m (6ft 6in), coupled with unduly slim columns of 5.7m (18ft 9in), would appear unimpressive if seen otherwise.

In plan the Hephaistion resembles the earlier temple of Zeus at Olympia in the Peloponnese, but is on half its scale,

measuring 31.7 by 13.7m (104 by 45ft). Possibly its carvings were influenced by those on the Parthenon, where work progressed more rapidly. The Hephaistion became a church in the 6th century AD, which explains why it is so well preserved. (Most temples were not converted to churches, chiefly because they were the wrong shape for Christian worship.)

ATHENS' LARGEST TEMPLE

The Pisistratids had started a gigantic temple to Olympian Zeus east of the Acropolis in c.520BC, its size reflecting both their dynastic pretensions and Zeus' status as supreme deity. They had got no further than its base before their expulsion in 510BC. For the next 350 years the site remained untouched until Antiochus IV, an energetic Seleucid king of Syria, paid for work to restart in 170BC. The architect was Cossutius, a Roman who had worked in the Greek east in opulent Hellenistic style. He continued with the basic plan but gave the temple gigantic columns of the Corinthian order. It was the first time this order had been used so grandly in Athens. But the temple was not completed as Antiochus' death in 164BC cut off funds. Sulla, the Roman general, removed some of the temple's capitals to Rome after sacking Athens in 86–85BC. Only when the philhellenic Emperor Hadrian visited Athens was the great temple finally completed in AD131. Hadrian's plan generally followed Cossutius' designs, but the standard of workmanship was not so fine. The columns are 16.7m (55ft) high and unusually proportioned, their height being equal to 8¾ of their lower diameter. The huge temple finally measured 108 by 41m (354 by 135ft).

THE TEMPLE OF POSEIDON

Very similar and probably built by the same unknown architect around 440BC is the Temple of Poseidon the sea-god. It is superbly sited at Sunium on the very tip of Attica. Though built of a less fine local marble, not pentelic, it shows the architect's skills developing. Its dimensions are similar to the Hephaistion's but the columns are 30cm (1ft) higher. Each column has only 16 shallow-carved flutes instead of the usual 20, removing the need for entasis. Whether seen by sailors rounding the cape or by worshippers approaching from land, the temple has always looked marvellous, gleaming hundreds of feet above the sea. It was built on the base of an earlier temple, which is thought to have beeen destroyed by the Persians in the invasion of 480BC.

BASSAE: A RADICAL INTERIOR

Equally impressive but very different is the Temple of Apollo Epikourius, Apollo the Helper, built by the small state of Phigaleia in Arcadia, the most rugged part of the Peloponnese. This was in thanks for divine deliverance from the plague, at least so wrote Pausanias 600 years later, who claimed that its architect was Ictinus who had just designed the Parthenon. But Apollo may have delivered the little state from foreign aggresion, not plague. *Epikouros* in ancient Greek can mean mercenary soldier.

The temple was probably started about 429BC and finished, after interruptions caused by Spartan occupation, in 400BC. Built of grey local limestone – at 1,127m (3,700ft) up amid mountainous ravines, Bassae is too remote to be supplied easily or cheaply with marble – the temple's proportions appear rather old-fashioned, with six by 15 columns. Externally it lacked most of the latest refinements such as entasis, which suggests that the builder was possibly a provincial.

However, its interior was remarkably radical, which suggests that Ictinus was indeed the real architect. Its cella is flanked by impressive Ionic half-columns

(sunk in the wall). Their bases are abnormally flared, echoing the flamboyant capitals. which have three-faced capitals with two volutes (scrolls) and curved tops. Most radical of all was a free-standing column with a Corinthian capital at the south end. (Originally there may have been two others. This column has since perished but is known from drawings.) Bassae is the first known use of the elaborate third order, which became so popular in the Hellenistic and Roman eras.

Above: The Temple of Olympian Zeus is the largest temple in Athens. Started in the 6th century BC, it was only completed in Hadrian's reign (AD117–138).

Below: The Temple of Apollo at Bassae in remote Arcadia was possibly designed by Ictinus, the Parthenon's architect, in 429BC.

THE WORLD'S FIRST THEATRES

Above: The vast theatre at Pergamum, capital of the wealthy Attalid kingdom in north-western Asia Minor, was carved from the steep acropolis side in the 2nd century BC.

Below: The theatre at Priene was small, suiting this tiny polis in Asia Minor. Built c.300BC, it is typical of many Greek theatres.

The Greeks built the world's first permanent theatres to stage their great plays. Athens, which pioneered drama and comedy in the 5th century BC, also pioneered the structural development of the Greek theatre. Its form then spread around the expanding Greek world and was finally taken over and adapted by the Romans. Greek theatres were always open to the sky, although March, the month of the Greater Dionysia and the annual drama contests, can be cold even in Greece.

Theatre in Athens began simply, using a natural hollow on the south slope of the Acropolis in the 6th century BC as its venue. This site was transformed over the next two centuries into the great Theatre of Dionysus, seating up to 17,000 spectators, and was embellished over the succeeding centuries into the Roman era. Classical plays are still performed in it, making it probably the world's oldest theatre still in current use.

THE FIRST THEATRE

The auditorium of the first theatre was a simple semicircle of wooden benches perched on the steep 1 in 8 slope. Below was a round dancing area, the *orchestra*, about 25m (82ft) across. Here the chorus danced and sang and actors, first one, then two and finally more, stepped out to declaim. A plain stone wall acted as a backdrop. After the Persian defeat in 479BC, Xerxes' resplendent royal tent, 60m (200ft) wide, was used as a backcloth for plays, according to tradition. (*Skene*, later meaning background building or scenery, originally meant tent.) Outside the theatre stood a small temple to Dionysus, the god of drama.

As the city grew, the semicircle of tiered seating was expanded further up and round the Acropolis' slopes. Pericles is credited with building the first stone theatre in the 430s BC, along with the smaller covered *odeion* but many archaeologists date the oldest stone remains discovered to after 400BC However, there definitely was a wooden skene to which scenery could be attached in the 5th century. By the mid-4th century AD the theatre had achieved the form we associate with a Greek theatre: a hemisphere of stone benches rising above the semicircular orchestra, with a long stoa behind the stone skene, on which stage 'machinery' could create sometimes elaborate special effects.

EPIDAURUS, THE PERFECT THEATRE

The most beautiful and best-preserved of Greek theatres is that of Epidaurus in the north-western Peloponnese. Although Epidaurus was not a polis of much importance, it constructed the archetypal Greek theatre on a clear, uncluttered slope. (In Athens, buildings and a cliff hemmed in the theatre.) Probably built by the

architect Polyclitus the Younger about 350BC, Epidaurus' perfectly symmetrical auditorium is 118m (387ft) in diameter and very nearly semicircular in plan. It boasts superb acoustics and also allows a good view from every seat – at least of the orchestra if not of the skene. The skene probably originally rose quite high. Later a proscenium, a structure jutting out from the skene, as the name suggests, was added on which actors performed. This suited the needs of the New Comedy, which depended more on individual characters interacting, less on grand choruses.

The stone seats are 76cm (2ft 6in) wide and 43cm (17in) tall. Like many ancient theatre seats, they are surprisingly comfortable. The best seats are in the centre low down. Two tall elegant doorways allowed easy entry and exit. The theatre seated about 12,000 people, a surprisingly large number for such a small city. It was probably seldom filled.

In the Hellenistic and Roman ages, theatres became steadily grander and more elaborate. That at Pergamum, capital of the wealthy Attalid kingdom, was carved dramatically from the steep acropolis side beneath the royal palace in the 2nd century BC. More typical was the theatre of Priene, which lay further south, a city rebuilt c.300BC, which resembles Epidaurus on a smaller scale. Here the skene had two storeys and a proscenium in front.

ODEIONS

All theatres were open-aired, seating many, sometimes all, the citizens, but covered buildings were erected for musical and literary events. Around 440BC, Pericles built the first odeion (from which comes our word 'odeum'), an immense covered building next to the theatre. Its wooden roof, topped by an open-sided lantern for light and ventilation but chiefly designed with acoustics in mind, was supported on 81 columns in nine rows. Reputedly, it too was modelled on Xerxes' tent, that paradigm of oriental luxury. The odeion hosted the musical and poetry contests at the four-yearly Panathenaic Games. Originally it had wooden benches but in the 4th century BC these were replaced by stone. Many cities later copied Athens' example.

Above: Epidaurus has the best-preserved and most beautiful theatre in the Greek world. Probably built by the architect Polyclitus the Younger c.350BC, its perfectly symmetrical auditorium has superb acoustics.

Below: Begun in the 6th century BC, the Theatre of Dionysus in Athens assumed its final form by the mid-4th century BC, when its tiers of seats and skene were completed in stone. Seating 17,000 spectators, it saw the premières of works by Aeschylus, Sophocles, Euripides and Aristophanes.

STOAS AND COUNCIL HALLS

Above: The Agora of Athens, the ancient heart of the city, showing the Stoa of Attalus, the only building of its kind fully restored, with the Acropolis in the distance.

Below: The Agora at Athens under the Roman empire, when it had become almost crowded wth monuments. The oldest stoas from the 5th century BC are on the right (the Stoa Poikile housing with paintings) with the 'Royal Stoa'on the left. The bulky buildings, like the Stoa of Attalus at the top, are Hellenistic or Roman.

While temples and theatres are the Greeks' most famous public buildings, they developed many other buildings for urban life. From the 6th century BC on, increasing numbers of Greek cities built stoas: long, open-sided, pillared porticos, usually sited around the Agora. Giving shelter against winter rains or summer sun, and often carefully angled to admit warming winter sunlight, stoas sheltered many aspects of city life, from shopping or dining to philosophy. One important school of philosophy even took its name from a stoa: the Stoics.

THE FIRST STOAS

An early small stoa designed solely for shelter was at the Sanctuary of Hera in Samos from the 7th century BC. However, the first significant stoa that we know of was the Stoa Poikile (painted stoa), erected on the north side of the Athenian Agora soon after the Persian defeat in 479BC.

It took its name from the paintings on its north wall depicting heroic episodes in Athenian history. Ranging from

Theseus' (mythical) war with the Amazons to the Battle of Marathon, Athens' first victory over Persia in 490BC, the panels were painted by three great artists of the classical period: Polygnotus, Micon and Panaenus. These were described by the travel-writer Pausanias 600 years later but have since vanished.

Stoas were subsequently built all round Athens' Agora. Just south-west of the Stoa Poikile was the Royal Stoa, called after the 'King Archon', by then a purely ceremonial official. Beyond that another grander stoa to Zeus Eleutherios (Zeus the Deliverer) was built in the late 5th century BC. This had Doric columns externally but used the Ionic order inside. It was divided into compartments for different activities, which possibly included law courts.

THE STOA OF ATTALUS

Further stoas were built around the other sides of the Agora, the grandest being the Stoa of Attalus, the wealthy king of Pergamum. He endowed Athens with his superb two-storeyed stoa in the 150s BC. This has been totally reconstructed in recent years, to give a good impression of how the stoa must have looked when brand new. The lower floor has Doric columns, the upper floor and the interior Ionic. This arrangement soon became very common, even canonical, not only for stoas but also for other buildings. Even the Colosseum in Rome follows this pattern.

Many cities in Greece and across Asia, such as Miletus, Ephesus, Antioch and Pergamum, built extensive stoas lining their agoras and sometimes running down their streets. An unusually long stoa was the 'South Stoa' at Corinth, built around 300BC. It was 160m (525ft) long with 71 Doric columns along its straight façade. On the gutter was a row of water-spouts in the form of lions' heads, each separated by an acanthus scroll, a common decorative device. Water gushed up from wells inside the stoa, coming from the springs of Peirene at the Agora's east end. When the Romans sacked Corinth in 146BC, they found and burnt in the stoa shops containing paint, clay, lime, along with much elaborate pottery. This suggests that workshops were located there, making stoas truly multifunctional.

BOULETERIA: COUNCIL HALLS

Although the Assembly (*ecclesia*), the sovereign body in democratic Athens, met in the open – with a quorum of 6,000 it had to – the far smaller Council did not. The Council (*boule*), of 400 or 500 councillors chosen annually by lot, discussed and shaped new proposals before they went before the often unpredictable full Assembly. But unlike the Roman Senate, the boule had little real power, at least when Athens was a full democracy.

In Athens the older Council Hall (*bouleuterion*) was a simple rectangular building on the west of the Agora, with a temple and document store attached. In the late 5th century BC a new bouleuterion was cut into the hillside behind it, with tiers of seats in a semicircle like a theatre, the old building now housing the state archives. A ceremonial porch was added 100 years later. Other cities copied Athens' example. The small island of Thasos had an almost square bouleterion, and Miletus a grand semicircular building for up to 1,500 people. This looked out on to a colonnaded courtyard in the Doric order, with a gateway with Corinthian columns beyond.

Among the largest bouleuteria was the Thersilion, built at Megalopolis in Arcadia. This new federal capital was founded late in 371BC after Sparta's long dominance of Arcadia had been ended by its crushing defeat at the battle of Leuctra. A rectangle measuring 86 by 67.7m (218 by 172ft), the Thersilion seated 6,000 people from all cities in the new confederate democracy. This meant a far bigger building than the Athenian

prototype. The centre of its front consisted of a series of doorways, but inside pillars were arranged to minimize obstruction between the speaker in the centre and his audience. The internal columns were unfluted Doric, and there was probably a lantern-type roof to admit light.

At Priene in Asia Minor a new bouleterion was built in *c*.200BC. Sunk into the slope like a theatre and seating 600 people – a high proportion of the tiny population – it was almost square, being 20.25 by 21m (64 by 66ft 6in).

Above: The bouleuterion (council chamber) of Priene, that model Ionian polis, was rectangular in shape, but many such chambers were semicircular.

Below: Attalus II, King of Pergamum, gave Athens a grand stoa in the 150s BC. Now totally reconstructed, it shows how such a stoa must have looked when new.

THE PRIVATE HOUSE

Above: In Delos, a thriving port in the 2nd century BC, rich merchants built fine houses with large courtyards that have survived remarkably well.

Below: The house of Diadomenus in Delos had a fine mosaic floor, a form of expensive but long-lasting decoration that would recur in many later houses in Italy.

In classical Greece, public magnificence was seldom matched by private affluence. Most houses in Periclean Athens remained modest. Citizens, who lived mainly in the open, happily spent their taxes (or their empire's tribute) on adorning their city, not their homes. But by the time Rome conquered Greece in the 2nd century BC, luxurious houses were being built in many places. These influenced Roman houses at Pompeii, that time-capsule buried by Vesuvius' eruption to give us vivid glimpses of antiquity.

Almost all Greek houses were built around courtyards with slits for external windows. Most in 5th-century BC Athens were built of mud-brick on a stone base and the windows had no glass. At first only the better houses had terracotta-tiled roofs, poorer ones using mud-tiles. Houses in Athens were crammed together without decent drainage or water supplies. For all its public splendours, classical Athens was not a salubrious city. Mud and filth clogged its narrow, mostly unpaved streets. However, some citizens always lived in markedly more lavish houses than others.

HIPPODAMUS OF MILETUS

Hippodamus (c. 500–420BC) is considered the first town planner and the inventor of the grid-iron plan. Although Smyrna had been rebuilt on a regular plan after an earthquake in the 7th century BC, Hippodamus produced the first coherent urban theories. He planned the Piraeus in the 460s BC, when it was growing fast, laying out regular-sized blocks for housing. An agora, approached by a wide avenue, was named after him. He then toured the Greek world, advising poleis from Rhodes to Thurii in Italy how to plan their cities. Others later copied his ideas. Sometimes, as at Priene, rebuilt around 330BC, Hippodamus' ideas were applied irrespective of the actual topography, which is steeply hilly at Priene.

ON THE ACROPOLIS' SLOPES

Demosthenes, the great orator (384–322BC), declared that luxurious houses were unknown before his time, but he exaggerated. Very comfortable houses from earlier decades have been found behind the South Stoa. All had courtyards and upper floors, with walls of mud-brick on a stone base and roofs of terracotta tiles. Halfway up the slope to the Acropolis, three houses built after 400BC have been discovered. The largest, measuring 25 by 19m (82 by 62ft) overall, had 10 ground-floor rooms and a large courtyard with a colonnade supporting a balcony. One room had a fine mosaic floor, which was clearly important because mosaics were rare. Opposite it was the *andron* ('men's room'), where men, reclining on couches, dined, drank and talked or were entertained by flute girls and dancers. Upstairs was the *gynaekeion*, the women's quarters –

women in classical Athens led segregated lives. The walls were painted with bands of colour. Similar houses have been found at the Piraeus and Megara.

FROM OLYNTHUS TO POMPEII

Olynthus, a city in northern Greece, laid out a new quarter on a rectilinear plan after 430BC. (Olynthus was destroyed by Philip II of Macedonia in 348BC.) Most houses, measuring 15.2m (c.50ft) square, had two floors, with cobbled courtyards at their centre and verandas on the north side to catch the winter sun. Their timber columns supported stone capitals on burnt-brick bases. Some houses had mosaic floors in the main rooms. The 'House of Good Fortune' has a superb mosaic made of 50,000 pebbles showing Dionysus driving a leopard-drawn chariot. Houses still had sun-dried brick walls on burnt-brick foundations, however.

Far grander houses were built after Alexander the Great's conquests, which enriched at least some people. At Pella, Macedonia's capital, houses 45m (150ft) square had larger rooms with peristyles (colonnades around a building) with stone columns. They also had bathrooms with terracotta bath tubs but had the same overall layout as at Olynthos.

The island of Delos, which boomed after Rome made it a free port in 166BC, saw Greek houses growing positively luxurious, but they still centred on an inner courtyard. Such courts now had peristyles all around and boasted elaborate mosaics, made no longer of pebbles but of finely cut stones. The roofs of these houses drained into the court and so into an underground cistern – Delos was chronically short of water. Comparable houses of the period have been found across the Greek world, from Dura in Mesopotamia to Saint Rémy in southern France.

Right: Most Athenian houses of the Classical period were relatively simple. On two floors, they centred around a courtyard, with colonnades supporting balconies on the upper floor and blank exterior walls.

Many of Delos' richest inhabitants were Italian businessmen. Through them, and through Greek artists or slaves imported into Italy, the 'peristyle house' spread to Italy. The best surviving examples come from Pompeii, where the peristyled courtyard of the House of the Gilded Cupids, built c.150BC, is so large that it is almost a colonnaded garden.

Above: The finest surviving examples of later Greek houses come from Pompeii, a city in Italy much influenced by Greek culture and preserved by Vesuvius' eruption. This is the House of the Vettii, dating from the 1st century BC.

CHAPTER II

BUILDING STYLES AND TECHNIQUES

The Greeks invented a classical language for architecture that has proved uniquely influential. The Romans later adopted and adapted the Greek style, exporting it across their own empire. The results of this artistic union, deliberately revived after 1400 in the Renaissance, shaped Western architecture into the mid-20th century. Greek architecture was trabeated, meaning it relied mainly on the column and lintel for its effect. This made the proportions of their columns, and of the entablature (the horizontal mass the pillars supported) all-important. The Greeks worked out canons (rules) for their different orders, or styles, of columns, which appear almost magically perfect. All were mathematically based, their proportions deriving ultimately from idealized versions of the human body. Classical architecture has retained its appeal because it appears supremely harmonious. It really is 'architecture with a human face'.

While Greek architectural theories and craftsmanship became sophisticated, building techniques generally remained simple. The Greeks seldom used cement, relying instead on metal clamps and precise fitting of stone, and had little machinery. But they were brilliant craftsmen in both stone and marble, working with supreme precision to create monuments of unageing intellect.

Left: The perfect proportions of the Temple of Poseidon above Cape Sunium exemplify Greek architectural skill.

BUILDING MATERIALS

Above: The Temple of Aphaea in Aegina is built of gleaming local limestone but was originally colourfully painted.

Below: The massive Temple of Athena at Poseidonia (Paestum) of the 5th century BC in southern Italy was once covered in stucco and brightly painted, creating an effect that is hard to imagine today.

While the Parthenon appears to float with effortless perfection above Athens, such excellence had taken the Greeks centuries to achieve. They started building not in marble or stone but in perishable timber and mud-brick. To create perfectly proportioned buildings, however, they needed to quarry, and work in, one of the finest if hardest of materials ever used: Greek marble.

The Minoans built their elaborate rambling palaces out of a mixture of adobe (sunbaked mud-brick), timber and rubble, usually stuccoed both inside and out. They had bases of stone or burnt brick needed to keep structures dry, and palaces built after 1600BC boasted walls of ashlar (cut stone). However, the Minoans' pillars were of wood and so combustible, as events catastrophically showed.

The Mycenaeans on mainland Greece used massive stones, often weighing 6 or more tons, to build their citadels at Tiryns and Mycenae. For these they hacked polygonal limestone megaliths ('big stones') from local hills. These were laid without plaster or cement on top of each other. This seemingly crude way of building was done so skilfully that it created the large tholos of the 'Treasury of Atreus'. Like Mycenae's cyclopean walls, it has lasted more than 3,000 years, But the knowledge and ability to build on such a scale vanished during the 12th century BC.

TERRACOTTA AND WOOD
In the Dark Ages (1100–800BC) the Greeks, when they built at all, did so in wood, making tiny temples with thatched roofs. Occasional early buildings, such as the first Temple of Hera, encouraged the use of terracotta (fired unglazed clay) roofing tiles (with wooden beams). At first these were very heavy, weighing up to 20kg (66lb). This led to the walls of the temple cella being made of stone and mud-brick, and finally also to stone columns. Well into the 6th century BC pillars were still often timber. (Later, wooden columns were widely replaced by stone ones.) Entablatures were also made of terracotta in the 7th century, before stone replaced it as a building material.

BUILDING IN LIMESTONE
The Greeks of the mainland and of Ionia were fortunate in having abundant limestone to hand when they began learning again how to build in masonry around 650BC. Comparatively easy to quarry and work, limestone can also be precisely chiselled, as the fine columns of the Temple of Aphaea on Aegina of *c.*500BC show.

In Sicily and southern Italy, where builders often had only much coarser materials, such as sandstone, to hand, temples were usually covered in stucco

and painted, as the entablatures of almost all Greek temples across the Mediterranean always were.

The first masonry was curvilinear. Blocks fitted together like a jigsaw puzzle in the 'Lesbian style' (named after some rustic-looking fortifications on Lesbos island). By 550BC Greek temples and public buildings were being constructed of polygonal megaliths of well-cut masonry. Private houses, in contrast, were long made of mud-brick on a stone base, but increasingly had fired-clay roof tiles. These were, of course, far more weatherproof than unfired clay.

MARBLE PERFECTION

Fine though limestone was, marble was manifestly finer, requiring more skill but giving crisper outlines. In the 6th century marble was increasingly used for adorning buildings – and by the century's end also for statues – but it was expensive to build completely in it. The main sources of good marble were Cycladic islands such as Naxos and Paros. Hauling slabs over the mountains to Delphi must have made even small marble temples such as the Treasury of the Athenians expensive, although it must have been cheaper in cities like Ephesus, near the sea.

But the great source of Athenian marble was local: Mt Pentelicum, 13km (8 miles) from Athens – a fact that helped make all the Athenian architectural achievements possible. About 25 ancient marble quarries have been identified on the slopes of the mountain. The first workings had begun by 550BC, but systematic exploitation took off only early in the 5th century. It peaked under Pericles' grandiose works programme after 460BC.

The crystalline rocks of Pentelicum produced the fine white marble used for most great public buildings in Athens, including those on the Acropolis. It superseded all other marble except that from Paros, which is easier for sculpting. The marble of the pediments was often painted or even gilded, so the effect would have been less blindingly white.

Although the rich golden tint that age alone gives to Pentelic marble could not often have been appreciated in antiquity, it was considered the world's finest building material by Greeks and Romans alike. Pentelic marble long remained one of Athens' principal exports. By the 2nd century AD it was being shipped not just to Rome but also to rich African cities like Lepcis Magna. In this way too, Greek architecture spread across the world.

Above: The brilliant white columns of the Erechtheum on the Athenian Acropolis were built of marble quarried from Mt Pentelicum nearby.

Below: The quarries of Mt Pentelicum, whose crystalline rocks produced the fine white marble used for Athens' great public buildings.

THE THREE ORDERS
DORIC, IONIC, CORINTHIAN

Above: Columns of the Doric order, first and simplest of the three Greek orders, or types, of column.

Above: An Ionic column, the second order, with its distinctive scrolled capital.

Below: A Corinthian capital, the last and most luxurious of the three orders.

Greek architecture is defined by its columns. Every Greek temple was enveloped in them, every stoa composed of them, every major public building flanked by them. Today the columns' descendants adorn so many nondescript banks and government offices that we may see them as mere decoration or just ignore them. But they had vital functional roles in Greek architecture. Even when not supporting roofs and entablatures, they expressed Greek beliefs in mathematical harmony and proportion.

Harmony and proportion, of course, are central to most architecture. Unusually, Greek architecture derived these, at least in theory, from the idealized human form. (Many Greek architects wrote books on architectural theory but none has survived. Only those by Vitruvius, a Roman architect of the 1st century BC, have, incorporating earlier Greek ideas.)

The Greeks used three orders, or types, of columns, distinguished chiefly by their capitals (heads). These are, in order of emergence: Doric, Ionic and Corinthian. The names supposedly reflect the orders'

origins. But while Ionic columns certainly first appeared in Ionian cities, Athens, also an Ionian city, employed the Doric order to wonderful effect on its Acropolis. Doric became seen as suitable for masculine or official buildings, Ionic as graceful and matronly or scholarly and Corinthian as charming and feminine. (The Romans added a fourth order, the luxurious Composite, and perhaps a fifth, Tuscan, a stubby form of Doric.)

THE DORIC ORDER
First, stockiest and seemingly simplest of the orders, Doric columns had no base. Like the wooden pillars they replaced, they rose directly from the ground. Doric columns, like all Greek columns, were 'fluted', having shallow concave grooves. At the shaft's top was the capital, with

Below: The British Museum in London was built in 1823–46. Its noble Ionic columns were inspired by the Temple of Athena at Priene. They show the perennial, highly flexible appeal of the Greek orders, with their mathematically based proportions.

an *abacus* on an *echinus*, or moulding (literally 'hedgehog'). On this stood the entablature, the whole horizontal stone mass, about a quarter the height of the column. Its lowest element was the architrave, a stone beam.

Above the architrave ran the frieze, composed of triglyphs and metopes. These may derive from carpentry: triglyphs, protruding blocks scored with three grooves, originated as ends of the crossbeams of a wooden roof. (Another view suggests that the Doric order was inspired by Egypt's all-stone temples.) The metopes, the slabs between the triglyphs, were often decorated with sculptures. Above ran the cornice, the topmost ledge of stone, and above that the pediment, the low-pitched triangular gable at the end of every temple and stoa.

Triglyphs were theoretically set over the centre of every column and over the centre line of every *intercolumniation* – the space between columns measured in *modules* (column diameters). Intercolumn-iation was crucially important in Doric temples. Architects normally allowed for five modules, but this caused problems with thicker columns. About 20ft (6m) proved the maximum span possible for an architrave, so at times extra columns were inserted.

THE IONIC ORDER
In the mid-6th century BC, the Ionic order originated in Ionia and the Cyclades. (It is probably not linked to the earlier Aeolic order, whose volutes, scroll-like adornments, grow from the shaft of the column, enclosing a palmette.) The Ionic order was distinguished from the Doric in several ways: its shaft was more slender; the column was often taller; it always had a base; and its capitals ended in volutes that resembled either rams' horns or papyrus plants, according to the observer. The Ionian order was sub-divided between 'Asian' in Ionia proper and the islands, and 'Attic', the order of the mainland, which had a more elaborate base. (The Romans favoured the latter,

which consequently become common across the Mediterranean.) The Ionic frieze has no metopes or triglyphs, so there were no problems with intercolumn-iation. Ionic columns were used from the late 5th century BC on, when elegance rather than power was desired, as in the Erechtheum (421–405BC) on the Athenian Acropolis.

THE CORINTHIAN ORDER
The last of the three Greek orders to emerge was the Corinthian order. Vitruvius attributed its invention to Callicrates, a 4th-century BC architect, but the order was used internally on the Temple of Apollo at Bassae in Arcadia before 400BC. A Corinthian capital is richly decorated with two rows of acanthus leaves and other pieces of vegetation. This is its chief distinction from the Ionic order, whose measurements it otherwise generally shares. One of the finest surviving examples of a Corinthian building is the Choragic Monument of Lysicrates in Athens. Dating from 334BC, this is a beautiful circular memorial.

Above, l to r: The three great orders of columns, Doric, Ionic and Corinthian, which adorned every Greek public building.

Below: The Monument of Lysicrates of 334BC. Its circular form and Corinthian columns inspired the British architect 'Athenian' Stuart.

BUILDING PROCEDURES AND TECHNIQUES

Above: To construct the Parthenon and the other temples high on the Acropolis, builders had to haul heavy cuboids of marble from the quarries of Pentelicum on rollers or in ox-carts.

The Greeks had no powered machinery of any sort and relatively few mechanisms employing human or animal muscle power. Nor did they have huge armies of slaves, as the Egyptian pharaohs had done. However, slaves certainly worked on the construction sites in small groups alongside free citizens, who might well be their masters. Records have survived detailing the payments made to the small building companies – almost all family-type businesses – who built the temples of the 5th century BC. This small scale makes the Greek, especially Athenian, architectural achievement all the more remarkable.

Instead, the Greeks relied on their intellectual powers and remarkably skilled craftsmanship to erect their buildings. Few details survive of their actual building techniques, however.

The builders of the temples on the Acropolis and other parts of Athens first had to transport their heavy cuboids of marble up to the site high above the city. The requisite blocks were cut to size at the Pentelicum quarries, but

ancones, small protruding handles, were left on their sides to allow them to be lifted by ropes. (Ancones were usually chipped off after building work was finished but some can still be seen on the Propylaea, where the outbreak of the Peloponnesian War in 431BC prevented the work's completion.)

The blocks were then transported by unpaved roads 13km (8 miles) to Athens. Transport was presumably by ox-cart – the Greeks never used horses for haulage because they had no suitable harnesses. Alternatively, wooden discs may have been fitted to the slabs on which they rolled. Most blocks were dragged up the steep slopes of the Acropolis like this.

CRANES AND MACHINERY

Cranes were almost certainly used to help raise the masonry up to the temples during construction, although no traces of such machinery have been found. Aristotle, the encyclopaedically knowledgeable philosopher of the 4th century BC, describes complex pulley systems, with two upright timbers joined at the top with a brace and spread at the bottom. (Vitruvius wrote of very similar devices being used in Rome in the 1st century BC. Technology advanced with painful slowness, if at all, in the ancient world, so the machinery was probably much the same.) Lifting power came from a windlass attached to the back of the frame.

The 46 Doric columns of the Parthenon's pteron (outer colonnade) were made of 11 drums of marble. These were lifted into place by cranes using the ancones on each side. The column's top section, which included the Doric capital with its abacus and echinus, had its 20 flutes cut into it before being heaved into place and secured by metal clamps. Probably the fluting was cut around the base of the bottom drum to

Below: Complex pulley systems, with two upright timbers joined at the top with a brace and spread at the bottom, as described by Aristotle, were used to help build the temples.

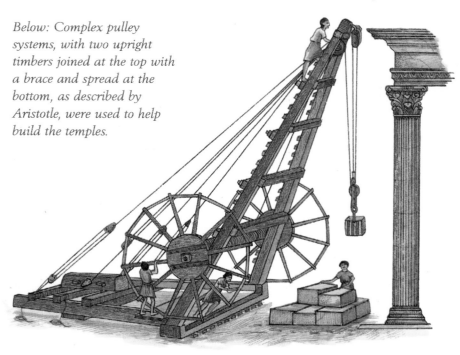

avoid harming the stylobate's paving. The rest of the fluting was carved after the column had been assembled on site.

'REFINEMENTS'

In building the Parthenon (447–437BC), Greek architectural 'refinements' – techniques designed to make temples appear perfectly proportioned from a distance – reached their climax. Foremost among these was entasis, the thickening of columns at the centre by 2.5cm (1in) one-third of the way up their 10.4m (34ft 4in) height. Corner columns, fully visible silhouetted against the sky, were 2.5 per cent wider than the other columns and leaned inwards. Similarly, the stylobate rises by 11cm (*c*.4⅓in) at the centre on each side, giving a marginally domed effect. The west end of the Parthenon was 44cm (17in) higher than its east end.

THE LACK OF CEMENT

One of the most remarkable aspects about the Greeks' construction techniques is that they never used mortar or cement until the Romans introduced it. Instead, they fitted their blocks with such precision on top of each other that their weight alone held them in place. In this way, Greek masonry resembles that of the Incas in Peru nearly 2,000 years later, who also created majestic and enduring buildings without mortar. The Greeks did use metal ties of iron or bronze to hold their massed masonry in place. Later generations pillaged many of these ties for their metals, particularly bronze ties, which were more valuable and less perishable than iron, so weakening the buildings. One technique that the Greeks employed instead of cement was *anathyrosis*, which probably originated in Egypt. This involves leaving the centre of the surface of each block rough and gently concave, while ensuring the edges were perfectly smooth, so creating a near-vacuum to hold the stones together.

LABOUR FORCE

All these refinements meant that there are almost no true straight lines of any length in the Parthenon, Hephaistion or many other Greek temples. As impressive as the mathematical knowledge needed for such calculations is the high level of craftsmanship involved. Compared with the pyramids or even some Greek temples in Asia Minor or the west, the Parthenon is not immense – its stylobate measures only 69.5 by 30.8m (228 by 101ft), but architecturally it is supremely accomplished.

How the Athenians assembled these temples, and indeed housed and fed the large, highly skilled workforce required to build them, so efficiently is unknown. They must have needed almost every skilled mason in Greece, which may have caused resentment among other Greeks. Certainly the use of taxes from the other poleis in their empire – which were originally intended for military purposes – to build temples for Athens' benefit alone was unpopular.

Above: For the Parthenon, heavy cuboids of marble were hauled from quarries on rollers or in ox-carts.

Below: Entasis makes columns look regularly spaced when seen from afar.

GATES, WALLS, WATER SUPPLIES AND SHIPYARDS

Above: The well-made but simple walls of the fort of Eleutherai, built c.400BC to defend Attica's western frontier, were typical of Greek defences for centuries.

Below: The walls built around newly liberated Messene in c.350BC were far more complex, having double gateways with enclosed courts in which enemy attackers could be trapped.

The Mycenaeans had built impressively massive and effective, if crude, walls. There was little further development in Greek city defences before 400BC, because there was no need. The Long Walls connecting Athens with the Piraeus, built in the 450s BC, baffled every Spartan attempt to take the city in the Peloponnesian Wars. The Peloponnesians had no success even when besieging tiny Plataea, having to starve the city out.

Similarly, when the Athenians attacked Syracuse in 414–13BC, they relied on building a wall to blockade the Syracusans. (Failure to complete this doomed the expedition.) Athens' own city walls, hastily rebuilt after the Persian wars, were c.2.5m (8ft) wide. A stone base of c.1m (3ft) supported upper walls of plastered mud-brick rising to c.8m (25ft). Towers c.5m (16ft) square reinforced the walls at key points.

In the 4th century BC, Dionysius I, tyrant of Syracuse, revolutionized siege warfare with his successful capture of Motya, a Carthaginian city off the coast off western Sicily, by using siege towers, causeways and catapults. Philip II of Macedonia and Alexander carried this revolution further. Alexander's capture in 332BC of supposedly impregnable Tyre, another massively walled island-city, signalled that cities must look anew to their defences. Over the next decades walls grew higher and thicker, to protect against missiles and to support catapults.

Towers, too, became larger and more frequent, with postern gates to allow sorties against besiegers. Semicircular towers, more costly to build but harder to attack, appeared in cities like Smyrna (Izmir) in the 3rd century BC. The towers of the small Ionian city of Perge were vaulted and had gabled roofs, presumably to keep torsion catapults dry.

The most famous defence of a city came in 305BC when Demetrius I, one of Alexander's flamboyant successors, failed to capture Rhodes after a year-long siege, despite assembling massive siege towers and catapults.

GATES

Athens' city walls had 15 gates. The most important, the Diplyon Gate, was elaborate, being of the 'courtyard' type. It was set back from the walls so that enemies exposed their flanks to javelins and arrows thrown by defenders on the towers and walls on either side. But the reasons for building such a grand gate like this were as much ceremonial as military. The great Panathenaic Procession entered the city by the Diplyon Gate, so it had to look impressive.

During the 4th century BC, gateways became more sophisticated. Double gateways with separated enclosed courts in which an enemy could be trapped were built at Messene c.350BC and Miletus c.300BC. The grandest such gate was at Pergamum, built c.200BC, which trapped attackers in successive enclosed courts.

WATER SUPPLIES AND SHIPYARDS

Adequate water supplies were clearly vital for any city. The Pisistratids about 530BC first brought water into Athens through rock-cut conduits piped from Mt Lycabettus north of the city. These supplied a fountain in the Agora, which was later roofed over. It had basins about 6 by 3m (20 by 10ft) at either end of a 18m (60ft) long building. The western basin was a reservoir into which vases

Below: A water conduit in Corinth, typical of many in which Greek cities channelled water through their cities.

could be dipped, the eastern end had spouts. This served as a prototype for other spring houses known from vases.

At Corinth, another important trading city, the 'Triglyph Wall', so-called because of its decoration, was built c.500BC above a spring chamber with steps leading down through an opening in the wall. More typical was the simple fountain niche such as that built into the walls at Priene c.330BC. Wherever possible, a large fountain was placed near the agora of each city. These gave women, who fetched the household water in amphorae balanced delicately upon their heads, a rare opportunity to meet and socialize.

Among Athens' grandest buildings were the naval shipyards at the Piraeus, essential to maintaining the fleet, for long the strongest in the Aegean. This had 372 shipyards in its final and grandest form. The huge fleet kept under cover could theoretically be launched very quickly. In practice, the Athenians lacked the crews to man all their ships when war finally came in 323BC. Athens' grandest naval building was the military arsenal built by the architect Philon in the 330s BC. It was a huge hall under a single-ridged roof. The interior measured 15 by 120m (50 by 400ft) and was 8.2m (27ft) high. It had a Doric frieze around the exterior and Doric columns, unusual for the time but meant to emphasize military strength.

Above: The defences of the small city of Perge in Asia Minor in the 3rd century BC boasted semicircular gable-roofed towers in which catapults could be mounted.

Below: The massive, if crude, walls of Mycenae, dating from the 13th century BC, were not surpassed as defences until the 4th century BC.

ELEMENTS OF ARCHITECTURE
GLOSSARY OF TERMS

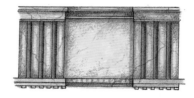

Above: A Corinthian capital, the most ornate of the three Greek orders, has a slender column similar to the Ionian order's but its capital has two ranks of acanthus leaves over the astragal, with caules rising over the acanthus leaves and sprouting volutes.

Above: Section of a Doric frieze showing how it is separately into blocks. The metope is the square space between the triglyphs, which have two vertical grooves (glyphs) in the centre and a half-groove at each end.

Our architectural language remains predominantly Greek in origin. Some words have passed into common usage but many others may seem obscure today, so a glossary of terms used in the book follows. They should prove useful for understanding not just ancient architecture but also many more recent buildings.

ABACUS Slab on top of a capital supporting the architrave

ACANTHUS Plant with scalloped leaves used as a design on Corinthian capitals

ACROPOLIS Upper or higher city, often reserved for temples and shrines in the Classical Age

ACROTERIA Plinths for statues or ornaments at the end and top of pediments

AGORA Market, forum or meeting place at the centre of every Greek polis, often with ceremonial colonnades around it

ARCHITRAVE Beam or lintel, usually in stone or marble, forming the lowest section of an entablature

BOULETERION Council hall

CAPITAL Head or crowning feature of a column

CARYATID Sculpted, clothed standing female figure used in the same way as a column to support an entablature

Above: A volute spiral is a decorative device used on Ionic columns.

CELLA Main body of a temple containing the cult image of the deity

CORINTHIAN ORDER Third of the Greek orders, with base, slender column and capital with two ranks of acanthus leaves

CORNICE Topmost horizontal, usually projecting part of entablature

DENTIL Small square block used decoratively in cornices

DORIC ORDER First of the Greek orders, without base (Greek Doric)

ECHINUS Moulding beneath the abacus on a Doric capital

ENTABLATURE Whole horizontal upper part of a building carried on columns above the abacus

ENTASIS Slight convex curve used on columns to correct the optical illusion of concavity when seen from afar

FLUTING Shallow, concave grooves running vertically on a column

FRIEZE Middle division of an entablature between architrave and cornice

GUTTAE Small projecting pieces under each triglyph of a Doric capital

Left and far left: Caryatids are draped female figures, supporting an entablature on their heads. The photo shows caryatids on the south porch of the Erechtheum in Athens.

Left: A pediment, such as this from the Temple of Artemis on Corcyra (Corfu) of 580BC, is the triangular space created by the sloping eaves and horizontal cornice of a gabled temple or other building or ceremonial gateway.

INTERCOLUMNIATION Space between columns, normally measured in their diameters

IONIC ORDER Second of the Greek orders, with voluted capital and base

MEGARON Large rectangular hall in Mycenaean palaces, and a possible influence on early Greek temples

METOPE Square space between two triglyphs in a Doric order, often sculpted

MODULE Unit of measurement, often diameter or radius of column at its base

NAOS Innermost chamber of a Greek temple. See CELLA

ODEION Covered hall, smaller than the main city theatre, used for performances of music and poetry

ORCHESTRA Dancing floor for the chorus in Greek theatres

ORDER All the parts comprising a column and its entablature. See Corinthian, Doric, Ionic

PEDESTAL Substructure under a column

PEDIMENT Triangular space created by sloping eaves and horizontal cornice of gabled temple or other building or ceremonial gateway

PERIPTERAL Of a building surrounded by a single row of columns

Left: The slight convex curve on a column is known as entasis and makes the column appear to be straight.

PERISTYLE Continuous colonnade surrounding a temple or court

PLINTH Low plain block under the base of a column or pedestal

PODIUM Continuous pedestal with base supporting columns

PORCH/PORTICO Roofed space forming the entrance to a building, normally with columns and pediment

PROCELLA Vestibule

PROPYLAEUM Entrance gateway to an enclosure, usually of a temple

PTERON External colonnade

SHAFT Trunk or body of column

STOA Shallow long portico with colonnade on one side, wall on other

STYLOBATE Continous base or plinth on which a row of columns is set

THOLOS Domed circular building, often a tomb in the Mycenaean Age

TORUS Convex semicircular moulding

TRIGLYPH Blocks separating the metopes in a Doric frieze, with two vertical grooves (glyphs) in the centre and a half-groove at each end

VOLUTE Spiral scroll at each end of an Ionic column

Above: The entablature is the upper part of an order showing, top to bottom, the cornice, frieze and architrave.

Above: The lower part of a column showing, top to bottom, the base and pedestal.

Left: Acroteria are plinths for statues or ornaments at the end or top of pediments (seen here on the Temple of Olympian Zeus). They were often highly decorated.

CHAPTER III

CITIES OF THE GREEKS

Greek cities developed from high Mycenaean citadels, beneath which small townships huddled, to cities on the plain or coast. As Aristotle noted, aristocrats and kings preferred high places, but democracies chose lower ground, reserving the acropolis ('high city') for the gods. Nowhere illustrates this transition better than Athens, the archetypal Greek *polis*, or city-state. Above, on the Acropolis, stood the temples of Athena and other tutelary deities. Down below were all the other temples, public and private buildings, theatres, stadia, altars, gymnasia, stoas, houses, prisons, tombs and monuments. The Agora (market place) was the focus of social, intellectual and political life; around it hummed the city's turbulent life.

By 500BC Greek colonization had spread Greek *poleis* around the Mediterranean, from Egypt to southern France. After Alexander's conquests (336–323BC), there was an even greater expansion of Greek *poleis* east to the borders of India. These, too, were (for a time) self-governing cities, with theatres, agoras and gymnasia. West of the Euphrates, Roman rule ultimately saved and furthered Greek urban life, as impressive ruins attest, but some very important cities – Sparta, Thebes and Alexandria – have left few visible ruins. Ancient Thebes is mostly under modern Thebes; Alexandria's ruins are practically all under water; Sparta built relatively little. So attention turns to the sites and cities that do survive.

Left: The buildings on the Acropolis, created in the 40 years after 446BC, help to make Athens the supreme Greek polis.

THE ACROPOLIS TEMPLES

Above: The small Temple of Athena Nike, the first temple seen by visitors approaching the Acropolis, was built c.428–425BC, very probably by Mnesicles.

Below: Pericles and other Athenians admiring Pheidias at work on the frieze that decorated the Parthenon, as envisaged by the Victorian painter Alma-Tadema in 1868. In reality, women would not have accompanied the men.

In the Bronze Age, Athens was of secondary importance compared to great centres such as Pylos and Mycenae. However its Acropolis, the rock dominating central Attica, is superbly defensible. Remnants of a Mycenaean palace have been detected on its north side. The citadel was enclosed in Cyclopean walls 6m (20ft) thick, fragments of which are still visible. The palace occupied part of the Acropolis, the lower town spilling out beyond the gates to the west, protected by an outer wall.

The legendary Erechtheus, one of Athens' first kings, established the worship of Athena in the city. His descendant Theseus killed the Cretan Minotaur, uniting Attica for the first time. Athens was renowned as the 'unsacked city', the one Mycenaean stronghold to survive 12th-century BC cataclysms. This may have been due to a secret well down eight flights of stairs inside the rock, which helped the city to survive long sieges. The last king, Codrus, traditionally sacrificed himself to save Athens from invaders.

The myth cloaks the facts. By c.950BC Athens had expelled its kings, and aristocrats ruled the city, but not from the Acropolis. They did so from the nearby Areopagus (Hill of Mars), which gave its name to their council. Athens in the Dark Ages and Archaic period (at least down to c.560BC) built no more temples in stone than any other Greek city. Only with growing prosperity in the early 6th century BC did the Athenians start to build again in stone. A wave of competitive construction soon led nobles to erect splendid monuments where all could admire them: on the Acropolis.

THE FIRST STONE TEMPLES

In 566BC the massive ramp leading up to the Acropolis was constructed by Lycurgus, a leading nobleman for the Great Panathenaea, the city's main festival. Other nobles, very probably the Alcmaeonids, sponsored the building of the first proper temple to Athena Polias. Decorated with painted snakes, bulls, lions and tritons, it was built of limestone and at c.30m (100ft) was twice as long as it was wide. Inside stood an ancient statue of the goddess, the city's most sacred object, evacuated to Salamis when the Persians invaded in 480BC. (The dating – even siting – of the Acropolis' early temples remains debatable.)

The Pisistratids, in power from 546 to 510BC, gave Athens a huge boost economically and architecturally. They moved the Agora to north of the Acropolis, giving it more space, and built nine marble drinking fountains; they embellished the Temple of Athena Polias with marble and began the vast Temple of Olympian Zeus. This was left only knee-high when Hipparchus, last of the dynasty, was driven out in 510BC. (The Pisistratids seemingly lived on the Acropolis in their last years in power.)

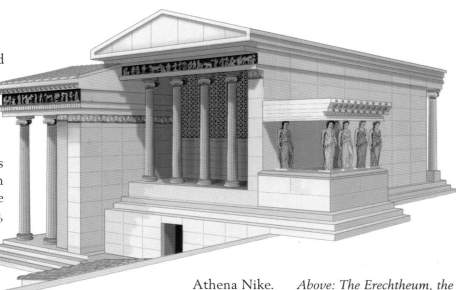

BUILDING FOR DEMOCRACY

The democratic revolution that followed halted the building programme only briefly. Victory over the Persians at Marathon in 490BC boosted the new democracy's self-confidence. A grand gateway to the Acropolis with Doric marble columns, the Propylaea, was started and perhaps finished. Even grander but unfinished was the large temple on the south side of the Acropolis, also in marble. The Persians burnt all these temples in 480–479BC and they remained unrestored for 30 years, although the Propylaea was patched up. Themistocles, leader during the Persian wars, oversaw the city's hasty refortification and the building of the Piraeus on Hippodamus' orthogonal (grid-iron) plans, but such buildings were purely utilitarian.

PERICLES' MASTERPLAN

Pericles had the very highest conception of his city, calling it the "school of Hellas", the exemplar of democracy at its noblest if not broadest. (It was a view shared even by some of Athens' traditional enemies. "O shining city, violet-crowned… Bastion of Hellas, glorious Athens, city of godlike men," wrote the Theban poet Pindar.)

More controversially, Pericles also thought that Athens was justified in using tribute money from the Confederacy of Delos, which had originally been intended solely for fighting the Persians, to rebuild its temples, themselves destroyed by Persia. The project that he persuaded the Athenian Assembly in 449BC to approve – after a long and stormy debate – would produce the grandest, most dramatic group of buildings Greece had yet seen.

Pericles chaired the committee overseeing the project, taking a keen interest in the work. Pheidias, the sculptor in overall charge, was his friend. Beneath Pheidias worked a team of architects. Ictinus was responsible for the Parthenon, Mnesicles for the Propylaea and probably the Erechtheum and the Temple of Athena Nike.

When completed (the Erechtheum, in some ways the most ingenious of all Athens' temples, was not finished until 405BC, the year of Athens' final defeat by Sparta at Aegospotomai), the grouped buildings, with their superb carved and painted friezes, astonished and awed contemporaries. Their feelings have been shared by most later generations.

Only in the Hellenistic and Roman periods, when absolute monarchs or emperors had far greater resources, would other architectural ensembles rival – and sometimes surpass – the Acropolis in size. None would ever surpass democratic Athens aesthetically.

Above: The Erechtheum, the last of the Acropolis temples to be completed, is really a multiple temple, housing 10 different shrines on two separate levels. It is named after Erechtheus, a legendary king of Athens.

Below: A reconstruction model of the Acropolis seen from the west, with its great staircase leading up to the Propylaea. Pheidias' statue of Athena rose just beyond this.

ATHENS' OTHER BUILDINGS

Above: The octagonal Tower of the Winds was designed c.454BC by the astronomer Andronicus of Cyrrhus. On its roof stood a large triton-shaped weathervane.

The splendours of democratic Athens were not restricted to its Acropolis. Down below, the Agora was surrounded from the 5th century BC on with increasingly fine official buildings. The old Bouleterion (Council Hall), a rectangular building about 23m (75ft) wide on the west side, was patched up after the Persian sack. It was replaced by a semicircular building better suited for meetings of the Council of 500, the advisory body, later in the century. The tholos, a domed circular building nearby c.18.3m (60ft) in diameter, was probably a clubhouse where councillors on duty ate their free dinners.

AROUND THE AGORA
On the north of the Agora the Stoa Poikile – Painted Stoa, called after paintings celebrating Athenian victories – was built c.470BC. It was the first such multi-functional structure. In the shelter of these extended porticos, citizens gathered to talk, listen and trade. Forty years later, the Stoa to Zeus Eleutherios (the deliverer) was built on the west side of the Agora. There was an altar to the 12 Olympian gods before it and the smaller Royal Stoa beside it. All had imposing Doric colonnades but were dwarfed by the huge, two-storeyed Stoa of Attalus, donated by the rich Hellenistic king Attalus II of Pergamum in the mid-2nd century BC.

Set back from the Agora, the temple of Hephaistus embodies all the principles of 5th-century BC Doric classicism, if lacking the 'refinements' of the Acropolis temples. More impressive due to its site but less well preserved, the Temple of Poseidon at Sunium is by the same unknown architect. So perhaps was the Temple of Ares, moved from Acharnae 24km (15 miles) away by the Romans. The huge Temple to Olympian Zeus, started under the Pisistratids, was half-completed thanks to Antiochus IV, the extravagant Seleucid king, with Corinthian rather than Doric capitals. Antiochus' death in 164BC abruptly ended work. Then Sulla, the Roman general who sacked Athens in 86BC for supporting Mithridates of Pontus, removed its capitals to Rome.

MONUMENTS
Athens was also a city of monuments. Most were erected not by the state but by rich individuals or families. Dozens of such monuments lined the Street of Tripods, one of the principal avenues.

Left: Famous partly due to its spectacular site, the Temple of Poseidon at Sunium is probably by the same unknown architect who built the Hephaistion in the Athenian Agora. Both temples embody the principles of Doric classicism in the mid-5th century BC.

Right: Athens grew around the Acropolis, where the city's finest temples stood, and the Agora below, the centre of social and political life. Walls enclosed the city, and Pericles' double Long Walls later linked it to Piraeus, the port.

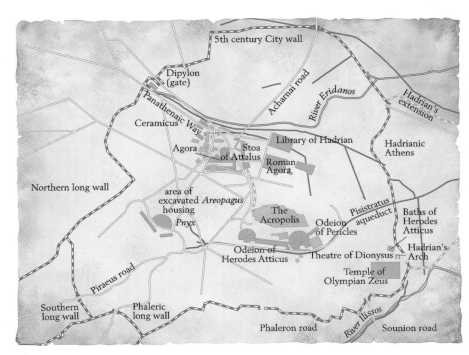

The most famous and elegant of these is the Choregic Monument of Lysicrates, built in 335–334BC. As a *choregos* (producer), Lysicrates had put on dozens of plays at his own expense – one of the duties expected of a rich citizen. This circular structure, with its slender Corinthian columns, proclaimed both his generosity and a victory in a theatrical contest. Its roof carried a three-branched acanthus on which stood a victory tripod. Its elegance has an almost Hellenistic air.

Yet the classical tradition remained strong in Athens, as another much later edifice demonstrates. The octagonal Tower of the Winds was designed *c.*45BC by Andronicus of Cyrrhus in Mesopotamia, a noted astronomer. Julius Caesar may have paid for it, for Athens as a city was almost destitute at the time. On its roof stood a large weathervane in the form of a triton, which pointed at the relevant wind, as personified in one of the eight wind zones. Inside was an elaborate water-powered mechanism that reputedly drove a sort of clock. Oriented due north, the tower carried sundials on each side so that passers-by could read the time on it. Like the Choregic Monument, it was made of marble and much admired by the British architect James 'Athenian' Stuart, who visited Greece in 1751.

ROMAN ATHENS

Roman rule, finally established after 31BC by Augustus, proved benevolent overall. A large new odeion was built and a new Agora, complete with Athens' first public lavatories. He commissioned a small temple to Rome and himself on the Acropolis. While admiring Greek classical culture, he stressed Rome's political authority. Nero refurbished the Theatre of Dionysus in AD61–4. But the real

philhellene was Hadrian (reigned AD117–38). He became archon (ruler), made Athens head of a Panhellenic League and built a new quarter with aqueduct and library. Herodes Atticus then restored the stadium for the Panathenaic games and built a vast new odeion beneath the Acropolis. His was the last contribution to ancient Athens.

Below: The two-storeyed Stoa of Attalus, built by the wealthy Attalus II of Pergamum in the mid-2nd century BC, is Athens' largest stoa, now reconstructed.

OLYMPIA AND EPIDAURUS
RENOWNED SANCTUARIES

Above: The entrance and grassy banks of Olympia's main stadium, where 40,000 spectators gathered for the great Panhellenic festival, held quadrennially for 1,200 years.

Below: A model of the sanctuary at Olympia housing the enclosure of the Altis, at the centre of which was Olympia's great Temple of Zeus. So many votive statues were erected over the centuries that the precinct became crowded.

Not every place of importance was a major polis. Some sites became famous through being the centres of particular cults. Among the greatest was Olympia in Elis in the western Peloponnese. The Olympic Games were held there quadrennially for almost 1,200 years and its Temple of the Olympian Zeus contained one of the Seven Wonders of the World: the Athenian sculptor Pheidias' last masterpiece, the gold-and-ivory statue of the king of gods. This was reputedly so huge that, even though seated, Zeus' head brushed the roof.

OLYMPIA

According to Pindar in the 5th century BC, the games were founded by Hercules, the muscular superhero. Traces of Mycenaean settlement have indeed been discovered at Olympia, but traditionally the Olympic Games were founded in 776BC. They soon became a Panhellenic event, attracting competitors from all over Greece. The games were held around the time of the second full moon after the summer solstice – meaning in practice late August or early September – the games imposed a rare truce on the otherwise constantly warring Greeks.

At the heart of the sanctuary lay the rectangular enclosure called the Altis. Three giant Doric columns of the 6th-century BC temple of Hera on its north side have been re-erected, but Olympia's main temple was that to Zeus, in the Altis' centre. One of the largest in mainland Greece, this had a stylobate made of huge stone blocks each *c.*2.75m (9ft) wide. About 63.9 by 27.7m (210 by 91ft), it was built by the local architect Libon between 470 and 456BC from soft limestone and was covered in stucco, with marble tiles, gutters and sculptures. It lacks the architectural 'refinements' of most contemporary Doric temples. This was possibly because Libon could not manage them.

The temple was destroyed by a huge earthquake in the 6th century AD. Only the drums of its columns remain *in situ*, but the well-preserved statues from its pediments rank among the finest of all Greek sculptures.

At the centre of the enclosure stood the great altar of Zeus. The area must have finally looked almost cluttered with 69 such altars. Just outside the south of the Altis lay the Bouleterion, with two wings united externally by a portico of 27 Ionic columns of the 3rd century BC. The east side of the Altis was lined with the Echo or Painted Stoa, rebuilt in the 4th century BC. Beyond that lay the Stadium, where the main Olympic events took place. It could accommodate 40,000 spectators, standing on raised banks. Its stone kerbs survive to give a vivid impression of this, the world's first great international stadium.

To the west of the Altis lay the Leonidaion, a large hostel for distinguished visitors built by Leonidas of Naxos in the 4th century BC, with an

open court 30m (100ft) square. North of that was Pheidias' workshop, a tall hanger-like building where his great statue of Zeus had been made, which itself became an object of wonder. (Its ruins were later quarried for a Byzantine church.) Just north of that stood the Palaestra, a colonnaded wrestling ground, and beyond that the Gymnasium.

Olympia thrived throughout the Hellenistic period and, despite Sulla's inevitable sack in 86BC, flourished under the Romans too. Augustus favoured it and Nero took part in the games, uniquely winning every single one – as the judges prudently decided. Hadrian later restored some buildings. The games were finally banned by the devoutly Christian emperor Theodosius I in AD393.

EPIDAURUS

Sited on the Argolid plain, Epidaurus emerged as an important sanctuary only in the 5th century BC. It was the shrine of the demigod Asclepius, son of Apollo. Asclepius had many attributes, the most famous being his medical powers. He could even raise people from the dead, but was killed by a jealous Zeus for his impiety. Asclepius' symbol of a staff with a serpent coiled around it has become the symbol of medicine. Of his temple, built *c.*420BC at the centre of the sanctuary, almost nothing visible remains.

To the south stood the great altar of Asclepius. Nearby was a tholos built *c.*370–340 BC by the architect Polyclitus of local limestone with marble ornaments. (Outside the shrine, of about the same date and wonderfully preserved, is the famous theatre.) Sick pilgrims would make visits to Epidaurus as if to a Hellenic Lourdes, sleeping the night in the *enkoimeterion* (sacred enclosure).

Right: The tholos built c.370–340BC *by the architect Polyclitus at Epidaurus is the best-preserved of the site's temples.*

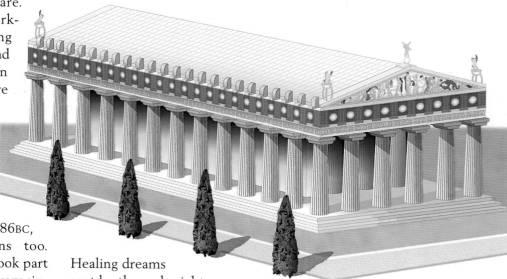

Healing dreams sent by the god might come to them there. Such psychosomatic cures could be very effective.

The Ptolemies of Egypt honoured the site, enriching it with offerings. Even the then-distant Romans sent to Epidaurus in 293BC asking for advice on a plague that was afflicting them. Despite the disapproval of the newly Christian imperial establishment after Constantine came to control all the empire in AD326, pilgrims in search of the god's help still visited the shrine well into the 5th century AD.

Above: The Temple of Zeus at Olympia, one of the largest in Greece, was built by the architect Libon of Elis between 470 and 456BC. It housed one of the Seven Wonders of the Ancient World: the huge chryselephantine (gold-ivory) statue of Zeus by the Athenian master-sculptor Pheidias.

THE SANCTUARY OF DELPHI

Nowhere was more sacred to the Greeks than Delphi. Apollo, the archetypal Greek god of poetry, reason and prophecy, had there slain (or tamed) the chthonic serpent Pytho, making the site his. To this *omphalos* ('navel', i.e. holy stone), centre of the Greek world, worshippers came for more than 1,300 years to consult the oracular priestess Pythonia.

From *c.*580BC on, Delphi was administered by the Amphictyonic Council, with representatives of several Greek states, including Athens and Sparta – the closest Greece got to a UN. However there were at least three Sacred Wars over the control of the sanctuary, the last war (356–346BC) leading to Macedonian hegemony under Philip II.

Above: The all-marble Treasury of the Athenians, built c.500BC by newly democratic Athens, was re-erected in 1906.

AN INTERNATIONAL REPUTATION

By the 6th century BC the Delphic oracle had gained an international reputation. Croesus, King of Lydia (560–546BC), sent to inquire if he should attack Persia. The reply, typically ambiguous – "If you cross the river Halys you will destroy a mighty kingdom" – led to his kingdom's downfall. The oracle's fame remained undimmed, however, the pharaoh Amasis also consulting it. Many Greek cities and individuals began building 'treasuries', in effect mini-temples, around the shrine.

During the Persian invasion (480–479BC), Delphi played an ambiguous role. When Xerxes sent troops to plunder the temples, the Persians reportedly were crushed by boulders hurled down by the goddess Athena Pronaia (guardian) from the surrounding crags. Probably this was a landslide, Delphi being a seismically active region.

The sanctuary is dramatically sited *c.*600m (2,000ft) up the slopes of Mt Parnassus. Approaching from the east up the Sacred Way, an Athenian would have come first to the sanctuary of Athena Pronaia, a Doric temple built *c.*500BC and damaged by the 480BC rockfall. Further up, a ravine separated the two *Phaedriades* (Shining Rocks) that reflected the light.

Here the Castalian Springs bubbled up, where Apollo had once planted his laurel tree, and here pilgrims purified themselves. Emerging, they would see the tholos gleaming above them, a round temple built *c.*375BC, with Doric columns outside and Corinthian ones within. This temple lay inside the *temenos*.

Left: The theatre at Delphi is one of the best preserved in Greece. Built in the 4th century BC, it was restored by Eumenes II of Pergamum in 159BC and again by the Romans. Its 35 tiers of seats are of white marble from Mt Parnassus.

The temenos (sacred precinct) of Apollo contained many buildings arranged to great effect against the landscape beyond. Among the treasuries was that of the Siphnians, dating from *c*.525BC, with caryatids instead of pillars. Beyond is the marble Doric Treasury of the Athenians, built *c*.500BC by the new democracy in gratitude for defeating its Greek enemies. The Treasury was re-erected in 1906. Its walls are covered with ancient inscriptions, some of which record Athenian athletes' victories in the quadrennial Pythian Games.

THE TEMPLE OF APOLLO

The largest building in the temenos was the Temple of Apollo, *c*.60m (200ft) long. The first temple, of the 7th century BC, burnt down in 548BC. It was replaced by a larger Doric temple with marble facings – then a luxury – financed by the Alcmaeonids, in exile from Athens. Wrecked in 373BC, it was rebuilt, sacked by Sulla in 86BC, and restored under the Roman Empire. The temple had six stuccoed limestone columns at the end and 15 on its sides, with an omphalos at its centre. Almost nothing remains.

The theatre above, by contrast, is one of the best preserved in Greece. Built originally in the 4th century BC, it was

restored by Eumenes II, King of Pergamum in 159BC, and again by the Romans. The 35 tiers of seats were of white marble from Mt Parnassus. The orchestra measured 18m (60ft) across, being paved with polygonal slabs. The front of the stage had a frieze depicting the labours of Hercules.

Above: The tholos, the round temple built c.375BC by Theodorus of Phocaea, has Doric columns outside and Corinthian ones inside, some of which were re-erected in 1938. It offers superb views.

Below: The stadium at Delphi of the 5th century BC. Here the Pythian Games, second only to the Olympic Games, were held every four years.

ENIGMATIC ORACLE

The oracle at Delphi retained its reputation for infallibility impressively long, partly through its excellent intelligence. Croesus tested the oracle by asking what he would be doing on a particular day. "Boiling turtles in cauldrons on a beach", came the reply, fed by inside sources.

But Delphi's real forte was its enigmatic prophecies. Pronounced in baffling verse 'interpreted' by priests, they often merely said, "Apollo thinks it better to…" This meant that, no matter how bad the outcome, the alternative would have been worse. It could pay to persevere. When the Athenians, facing Persian attack in 480BC, asked the oracle's advice, the first reply was chilling: "Fly far, far away; Leave home, town and castle, do not stay." Athens' envoys, returning for a better prophecy, were told to trust in the "wooden walls" but warned: "Divine Salamis will destroy the children of women." Themistocles spun this to mean that Athens should rely on its fleet – correctly as events proved. Julian, Rome's last non-Christian emperor (reigned AD361–3), received a depressing reply when he consulted the oracle, perhaps because it had been bribed by the Christians. Delphi was finally suppressed in AD384.

CORINTH
COMMERCE AND LUXURY

Above: The Fountain of Peirene, once a natural spring, was so built up over the centuries that it now looks like an ornamental fountain. The present façade was built under the emperor Claudius (AD41–54).

Below: The lofty citadel of Acrocorinth has been a key fortress in Greece for millennia. The present walls are mostly medieval but have Hellenic and Bronze Age foundations.

Superbly sited controlling the Isthmus, with access to sea routes east and west, Corinth was inhabited from earliest times. It took the lead in founding western colonies such as Corcyra (Corfu) and Syracuse in 734BC. Corcyra proved a disobedient daughter and the first recorded naval battle occurred in 664BC between it and Corinth. Under Periander (reigned c.629–585BC), Corinth boomed, exporting fine pottery around the Mediterranean. By the 6th century BC the city was already noted for its luxury, a reputation it never lost. The Corinthian order, most ornate of the three Greek orders, traditionally originated there, while Corinth's 1,000 sacred prostitutes, servants of the goddess Aphrodite, were renowned for their beauty and skills.

The Greeks' headquarters during the Persian invasion, Corinth was an often unhappy ally of Sparta's alliance. Later, Corinth was the site of Philip II's Congress in 338–337BC, where he proclaimed his planned crusade against Persia. It was also the last home of the philosopher Diogenes, whose world-renouncing eccentricities were the very antitheses of Macedonian megalomania.

Acrocorinth, the citadel rising 548m (1,800ft) above the city, then became one of the 'chains of Greece', garrisoned by Macedonian troops. Joining the Achaean League, which had liberated it in 243BC, Corinth was razed to the ground by the Roman general Lucius Mummius in 146BC. In 44BC Julius Caesar refounded the city as capital of the province of Achaea and it boomed again, its population reputedly reaching 300,000. St Paul preached in Corinth, appalled by its depravity but finding a readier audience among its merchants than among Athens' intellectuals. Despite recurrent earthquakes, Corinth retained its importance until the end of the Roman Empire.

Ancient Corinth lay on a rocky plateau 60m (200ft) high between Acrocorinth and its port Lechaion, connected by long walls. The ruins we see today are more Roman than Greek, however. The Lechaion Road, 12m (40ft) wide and paved under Augustus, led up past a colonnade of shops and the Peribolus (courtyard) of Apollo, toward the Fountain of Peirene. Originally a natural spring, this was so built up over the centuries that it resembled a large ornamental fountain. Water for it was stored in four reservoirs fed by a tunnel and hidden by a six-arched façade "with chambers made like grottoes, from which the water flows into a basin in the open air", according to Pausanias, writing c.AD170. This basin is 9 by 6m (c.30 by 20ft).

The present two-storied façade, built under Claudius (AD41–54), replaced a row of Ionic columns of the 3rd century BC. Herodes Atticus, a munificent multi-millionaire, remodelled the fountain into its present imposing vaulted and marble-lined form around AD150.

Above: The Temple of Apollo, north of the Agora in Corinth, is one of the oldest Doric temples. Dating from c.550BC, it has seven massive columns still standing.

A HUGE AGORA

Entered through the Propylaea, which the Romans turned into a triumphal arch, the huge Agora is itself really a Roman forum measuring 210 by 90m (230 by 100 yards). West of the Propylaea stood the Captives' Façade, an ornate two-storeyed marble structure. With Corinthian columns on the lower floor and Atlantes (giant figures) of barbarian captives on the upper, it dates from c.AD100. Nearby is the Triglyph Wall of stucco-faced lime-stone, reputedly built by the great sculptor Lysippus in the 4th century BC. This guards the Sacred Spring, which was origi-nally in the open but is now underground.

Stoas and temples line the Agora, with the Julian Basilica to the east and the South Basilica on the south – both Roman buildings. Also Roman are many of the small temples on the west side – including a Temple to Tyche (Fortune) and a little square Pantheon – the public baths and latrines. The Romans remodelled

the theatre, originally a 5th-century BC building, and carved the Odeion from the rock. But the Temple of Apollo on a hillock north of the Agora is wholly Greek, one of the oldest Doric temples from c.550BC, with seven austerely massive columns still standing.

ISTHMUS: CANAL AND GAMES

On the Saronic (east) side of the isthmus lies Isthmia, with the ruins of a 5th-century BC Temple of Poseidon. Here the Isthmian Games, traditionally founded by Theseus, King of Athens, and ranking just behind the Olympic and Pythian Games in prestige, were held every two years. Here also Alexander the Great was nominated leader of the Greeks against Persia in 336BC.

Just north lie the remnants of the Isthmian Wall, built against the Persians in 480BC, and beyond lies the Corinth Canal. This dates from only 1882, but the idea of a canal goes back to the 6th century BC, when Corinthians used to drag small ships across the Isthmus on rollers. At Nero's orders, work began in earnest on a canal in AD67, his engineers getting as far as the bedrock before stop-ping, defeated.

Below: The emperor Nero ordered the cutting of a canal through the Isthmus in AD67, a project the Greeks had long dreamed of, but his engineers stopped when they hit bedrock. Today's canal dates from the 19th century.

PERGAMUM AND PRIENE
CONTRASTING CITIES

Above: The theatre of Priene, dating from the later 2nd century BC, *is a perfect example of a Greek theatre. It has a two-storeyed skene building, providing fixed architectural scenery at ground level.*

Below: Pergamum developed around its Acropolis, once a citadel, whose height emphasized its architectural drama. The theatre is in the foreground.

Pergamum, once a small hilltop citadel, became under its Attalid kings (241–133BC) a marvel of Hellenistic town-planning. Its theatre, temples, palace, altars and library were dramatically arranged along the summit and sides of its Acropolis to rival Athens'. Yet Pergamum was no free polis but an absolute monarch's grand capital. In it the king's word was law, although the Attalids, who prided themselves on their philhellenism, shrewdly allowed Ionian cities under their rule autonomy. Their last monarch bequeathed his kingdom to Rome in 133BC. If smaller than the greatest Hellenistic capitals Alexandria or Antioch, Pergamum, unlike them, largely survives, although its major monuments have been mostly removed.

The first kings built only modestly, but after 200BC close alliance with the rising power of Rome meant a vast growth in Pergamene power and wealth. The upper city, broadly crescent-shaped, was spread over the southern slopes of a hill that, contracting as it rises, ends in a ridge a few hundred feet wide. Here was sited the Acropolis, necessarily irregular in shape, facing west.

Above: The Temple of Athena Polias at Priene was a sublime Ionic temple. Designed by Pytheos, it was dedicated in 334BC by Alexander the Great.

AT THE ACROPOLIS' FOOT

Beneath the Acropolis lay the lower Agora, a large enclosed court. Beyond it, running north, was a huge Stoa 213m (c.700ft) long, supported by a retaining wall. At the Stoa's north end, a small temple was rebuilt by the emperor Caracalla in AD214. Scooped out of the hill above it was a vast theatre, partly rebuilt by the Romans. Above to the east was the imposing temple of the emperor Trajan of the early 2nd century AD – Pergamum remained important under the Romans. Behind Trajan's temple lay barracks and the relatively small royal palaces.

The small Temple of Athena, built in an old-fashioned Doric style, stood in a large colonnaded courtyard. On the court's north side was Pergamum's famous library, second only to Alexandria's in repute, housing 200,000 scrolls. Parchment, the tough writing material made from hides, was traditionally invented in, and named after, Pergamum. Parchment was intended to counter Egypt's monopoly of papyrus, then the commonest writing material. Ultimately it replaced it.

THE ALTAR OF ZEUS

Between the Temple of Athena and the lower Agora rose the melodramatic Altar of Zeus. Built by Eumenes II *c.*165BC, it was one of the grandest, most resplendent structures of its age, although large altars had been built earlier at Samothrace and Syracuse. From the front the building appeared as a U-shaped Ionic colonnade on a podium with a huge sculptured relief. A vast flight of steps led up to the altar itself, which was architecturally insignificant compared to its surrounds. Most notable was the sculpted gigantomachia (battle of giants) on the podium, symbolizing Pergamene victories over barbarous Celtic invaders. (This flamboyant altar later struck the Christian author of Revelations [II, 13] as "Satan's Throne".) The whole upper city was enclosed by stone ramparts. In the lower city, ordinary people lived in simple mudbrick houses, as they did in many other Greek cities.

PRIENE: AN IDEAL POLIS

A total contrast to opulent Pergamum was Priene in southern Ionia. A tiny polis with a population of *c.*4,000, it was slowly but completely rebuilt from 334BC on. Aristotle and Plato, those so often differing philosophers, would have agreed that Priene had the ideal size and form for a true polis. Occupying a terraced sloping site south of its almost inaccessible Acropolis 300m (1,000ft) above, Priene was laid out on the orthogonal principles of Hippodamus. This ignored the mountainous actuality of its site. Six main streets 4m (13ft) wide ran east–west on level ground, crossed at right-angles by 15 streets climbing sometimes very steep gradients.

Near the city's centre, its Agora was entered via an arched gateway of *c.*150BC. This is the first Greek ornamental arch.

Right: Pergamum's upper city, broadly crescent-shaped, was spread over the southern slopes of a hill that, contracting as it rises, ends in a ridge a few hundred feet wide.

It is far less pompous than Roman triumphal arches, which almost invariably celebrate military triumphs. Around the Agora, public buildings included a fine *dipteral* (two-rowed) stoa with Doric columns outside and Ionic columns inside. South of the Agora lay the Stadium and Palaestra (wrestling school), to the north was the theatre. The first theatre, dating from 300BC, was replaced in the later 2nd century BC with a two-storeyed scena building. This provided fixed architectural scenery at ground level with upper wooden scenery.

The Temple of Athena Polias lay northwest of the Agora. A sublime Ionic temple designed by Pytheos, it was very possibly dedicated in 334BC by Alexander the Great himself, then liberating Ionia from Persian rule. Its six by 11 columns stood on square plinths with 24 deep flutes. Capitals have the classic egg-and-dart decoration on their echinus.

The temple was designed in the proportions of a Greek human foot (which is somewhat shorter than a modern foot), on a width/length ratio of 1:2. Such perfect proportions suit so perfect a polis, creating a perfectly balanced building.

Above: The theatre at Pergamum, dramatically carved from the steep hillside beneath the Acropolis, reflected the general flamboyance of the Attalid dynasty.

SYRACUSE AND ACRAGAS
SICILIAN CITIES

Above: The grand theatre at Syracuse, dating back to the 5th century BC. It could seat 15,000 people, revealing the city's size and wealth under its democracy.

Below: Part of the impressive fortifications around Syracuse that were brought to their peak by Archimedes, the city's most famous son, and that for long successfully defied the besieging Roman army under Marcellus in 212BC.

Ancient Sicily has been called the Greek America, for its fertile land was potentially very rich. Such wealth let the western Greeks build cities with unprecented splendour and distinction, if not always with great aesthetic subtlety. Sicilian cities' ruins are among the best-preserved in the Greek world but their politics were often ruinously unstable.

SYRACUSE

Founded in 734BC on the superbly defensible Ortygia island, Syracuse was already wealthy in the 6th century BC, as the massive if simple columns of its Temple of Apollo show. It rose to power under the tyrants Gelon and Hieron I (485–467BC). Gelon routed Carthage in 480BC and Hieron transplanted other Greek cities' populations to Syracuse. Both tyrants built lavishly. A superb Doric temple to Athena (Minerva) from their era survives, with 14 columns embedded in the walls of the current baroque cathedral. Its doors were covered in gold and ivory and on its roof a golden statue of Athena acted as a beacon to sailors. It is notable for sophisticated intercolumniation. The city's first theatre, trapezoidal in shape, was built beneath the present one. A fountain to the nymph Arethusa helped supply the city with drinking water and provided almost the only source of papyrus, the Greek paper, outside Egypt.

The city became a democracy after Hieron's death and as such repelled the Athenians' great siege in 415–413BC. But when attack by Carthage in 405BC threatened the city, a soldier called Dionysius made himself tyrant. Under his tyranny – which was truly despotic but lasted until 367BC – Syracuse attained new splendour, gaining extensive walls on the heights of Epipolae, that made it almost impregnable. But it lost not only its liberties but also part of its essential Greekness, many non-Greek mercenaries being settled there. The subsequent reign of Dionysius II (367–344BC) led to endless civil wars that wrecked Sicily.

HIERON'S GOLDEN AGE

In the 3rd century BC Syracuse regained its wealth under the steady rule of Hieron II (269–215BC). Its superb theatre was constructed then, as was its immense altar, which at 198m (650ft) was the longest ever built. Hundreds of animals were sacrificed on it at a time – Greek religion could be gory. Hieron patronized the poet Theocritus and the scientist Archimedes, who further strengthened the city's fortifications. But these did not prevent the Romans capturing the city after a long siege in 212BC when it had rashly supported Hannibal in the Second Punic War. Archimedes' accidental killing by a Roman soldier in its sack symbolized the end of Syracusan glory. Despite this, Cicero could still praise it in the 1st century BC as the elegantly Greek capital of the Roman province of Sicily.

ACRAGAS

Founded in 582BC in western Sicily from Gelon, another Sicilian city, Acragas (modern Agrigento) soon became one of the richest cities in the Mediterranean, thanks to its fertile territory and trade. In 488BC Theron became its tyrant. He continued work on the vast Temple of Olympian Zeus, one of the largest and most unusual of Greek temples, with its Atlantes, giant figures half-buried in the walls. After Theron had provoked Carthage by seizing Himera in 483BC, his alliance with Syracuse helped defeat the resulting Carthaginian attack. Victory led to an influx of slaves, allowing Acragas to expand work on the magnificent 'Valley of the Temples'.

This parade of Doric temples is now a UNESCO World Heritage site. Best-preserved of its temples is the Temple of Concord, built *c*.430BC of a local limestone so rough that it precluded many 'refinements'. With 13 by six columns, whose height equals 4.61 times their lowest diameter, it measures 39.4 by 16.9m (122ft by 18ft 6in).

After Theron died in 472BC, Acragas became a democracy, led in the 440s BC by the aristocrat, philosopher and radical democrat Empedocles. At its zenith, Acragas' population reputedly reached 200,000, rivalling Athens. Its inhabitants had luxuriously soft beds, elaborate fishponds and even pet swans. The poet Pindar praised it as the "most beautiful of cities inhabited by mortals".

But Acragas' good times did not last. When Carthage's war of revenge began in 406BC, the Acragantines, despite help from Syracuse, proved incapable of effective resistance. They had become so soft that even soldiers on sentry duty at night reputedly demanded two pillows, a mattress and quilt. In 405BC the city was

abandoned to the Carthaginians, who sacked but did not destroy it. Later it was repeopled by Timoleon, the saviour of Syracuse, in the 330s BC.

Acragas suffered badly again in the First Punic War (264–241BC). The Romans, capturing the city after a long siege, enslaved the whole population. Under the Roman Empire, Acragas finally regained a modest prosperity, but as a minor provincial town, not a great city.

Above: The great Doric Temple of Concord at Acragas dates from the 5th century BC, the city's golden age when it was reputedly the richest city in the Greek world, home of the mystical philosopher and statesman Empedocles.

Right: A fountain to the nymph Arethusa supplied Ortygia, Syracuse's inner city, with drinking water and provided almost the only source of papyrus, the Greek paper, outside Egypt.

DELOS AND EPHESUS
DIFFERING FATES

Above: The Library of Celsus at Ephesus, noted for its projecting pavilions, dates from c.AD110, when the city was thriving in the long Roman peace.

Two Aegean sites, both very closely connected with Greek life, sacred and commercial, had very different fates.

DELOS

A tiny island in the central Cyclades, Delos was the mythical birthplace of the god Apollo and his sister Artemis, among Greece's holiest shrines. 'Long-robed Ionians' with their wives and children gathered to honour Apollo at the annual *Delia* festival. At first, nearby Naxos dominated the island, donating the fine if much-weathered marble lions from c.630BC. Athens, the mother Ionian city, played a major role at Delos from the 6th century BC on and Pisistratus 'purified' the island in 543BC. Persia respected Delos' sacred neutrality during the Marathon campaign in 490BC, but in 478BC the Ionians, under Athens' leadership, based their anti-Persian League at Delos. In 426BC Athens ordered another purification, forbidding births or deaths on its sacred soil, banishing all Delians. From then on,

Athenian officials governed the island shrine. Delos became independent in 315BC after Athens' defeat by Macedonia.

Soon it was thriving as a trading centre, building a new theatre and temples. Among these the little Temple of Isis of c.170BC reveals both the persistence of the Doric style and the presence of Graeco-Egyptians resident in Delos.

THE SLAVE EMPORIUM

But Delos could not escape Roman power. In 166BC, Rome, to curb Rhodes, made Delos a free port. Soon the island filled with Italian merchants who made it the centre of the booming slave trade and built their own agora. Ever larger houses and monuments were erected. The boom ended with the sack by Mithridates' forces in 88BC, killing thousands of Italian merchants. The island then sank into obscurity. Pausanias in the 2nd century AD noted that the shrines' guards were almost the only people on the island.

The religious centre of the island was the Hieron of Apollo, the sacred precinct enclosing temples and altars. A vast 7th-century BC statue of Apollo stood on the north side, but only its base survives. The Great Temple of Apollo, begun in 477BC and completed 200 years later, had a high granite base with 13 marble columns down its sides. A Doric temple, it measured 19.5 by 13.4m (97 by 44ft). To the north lay the Sacred Lake, now dry, where Apollo and Letis were born. (Delos, now treeless, once had poplar groves.) To the south lay the theatre and around it luxurious peristyle houses with mosaics and

Left: In AD118 Publius Quintillius erected the monument known today as the Temple of Hadrian, dedicating it to Hadrian, Artemis and the people of Ephesus. It shows how Greek classical architecture could be adventurously enlivened with Roman arches.

fine columns, such as the 'Maison des Masques'. Similar houses have been well preserved at Pompeii.

EPHESUS

Traditionally founded by Ionian colonists on the coast of Asia Minor in *c.*1000BC, Ephesus was actually even older, having been a Mycenaean settlement. It went on to become one of the greatest of all Greek cities, a home of the Ionian Enlightenment (the enigmatic philosopher Heraclitus was born there) and a wealthy port.

Above all, it became famed for its great Temple of Artemis (Diana), one of the Seven Wonders of the Ancient World. The first temple, paid for by Croesus, King of Lydia *c.*560BC and designed by Theodorus of Samos, measured 109.2 by 55m (358 by 171ft). Originally made of limestone covered in marble, it had giant Ionic columns 20m (65ft) high. (The other Seven Wonders were the Pyramids, Alexandria's *pharos* (lighthouse), Babylon's hanging gardens, the Mausoleum of Halicarnassus, Pheidias' statue of Zeus at Olympia and the Colossus of Rhodes.)

Within its cella stood a statue of Artemis shown not as the usual chaste huntress of Greek mythology but as a many-breasted fertility goddess, suggesting possible Asian origins. The devotees of this Artemis were enraged when St Paul, visiting the city in the 40s AD, tried to attack their profitable cult. The sellers of religious trinkets rioted, crying: "Great is Diana (Artemis) of the Ephesians."

Ephesus suffered from the depression that hit all Ionian cities after the Persian wars, but recovered in the 4th century BC. Alexander's conquests made it a terminus for traders coming down the Meander from Asia. Resited in the early 3rd century BC (the old harbour was by then silting up) it continued to flourish, whether as a fully independent polis or under Seleucid or Attalid suzerainty. A new theatre at the foot of Mount Pion seating 25,000 was built *c.*200BC. But unwilling involvement in the wars of the Roman Empire after 130BC damaged the city.

However, in the *pax Romana*, the long Roman peace following Augustus' victory in 31BC, Ephesus flourished again as the capital of the wealthy Roman province of Asia (western Turkey). From this period, when Ephesus' population reached 250,000, date many grand buildings: the colonnaded street the Arkadiane, running through the city like a huge double stoa; the Temple of Hadrian; the Library of Celsus, noted for its projecting pavilions, and the opulent marble baths by the harbour. These show cosmopolitan Ephesians happily adopting the Roman arch and vault. Ephesus remained important into the early Byzantine era.

Above: The fine theatre at Delos dates from the 3rd century BC, *when the island was enjoying a prosperous independence as the centre of an island confederacy.*

Below: The 'Agora of the Italians' at Delos dates from the 2nd century BC. *The island, by then effectively under Roman rule, became the greatest slave emporium ever known, reputedly handling up to 10,000 slaves a day.*

CHAPTER IV

SCULPTURE

In the two centuries after 500BC, Greek sculptors created an art in which gods came to look like perfect human beings and humanity like incarnate gods. This art, simultaneously naturalistic and idealized, became the paradigm to which Western artists have recurrently turned. It also influenced non-Western art as far away as India. Greek sculptors focused on depicting the human form, often nude. Until after 400BC this meant exclusively nude males. While Greek men exercised naked in public, Greek women were cloistered away fully clothed. (Only in Sparta, nearly as devoid of art as it was of freedom, could female nudity sometimes be glimpsed.) Even when artists discovered the female nude in the 4th century BC, the heroic male nude still dominated Greek art.

A common misconception is that Greek sculpture was of lifeless white marble. In fact, many materials were used: limestone, terracotta, marble, wood, sometimes *chryselephantine* (wood covered in gold and ivory) and above all bronze. All were painted in lifelike colours, with eyes, lips, teeth and hair picked out so realistically they must have looked startlingly alive. Bronze, a valuable metal, was often melted down in the Middle Ages. Few of the great bronzes mentioned by ancient writers survive, although some statues have been found underwater. Instead, we must turn to later marble copies made for Romans, or images on coins or fragmentary carvings. Only the Elgin Marbles, original sculptures taken from the Parthenon, convey fully the lithe splendour of Greek sculpture.

Left: This majestic bronze of Zeus was rescued from the sea. Idealized yet also naturalistic, it dates from c.465BC.

MINOAN AND MYCENAEAN SCULPTURES 1700–1100BC

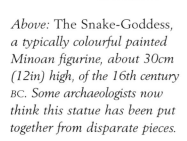

Almost no large statues survive from the Aegean late Bronze Age, when the Minoan and Mycenaean civilizations flourished. Possibly no statues of any size were ever made in Crete and the islands. Greek-speaking Mycenaeans (Homer's Achaeans) ultimately conquered Crete politically, but Minoan Crete conquered Mycenae culturally.

BULLS WITH GILDED HORNS

Minoan influence is often so overpowering on Mycenaean art – though not its architecture – that some archaeologists once posited a Minoan mainland empire. However, we now know that the influence came from Minoan artists or artists trained in Minoan techniques. This is revealed in two carvings of bulls' heads. (The cult of the bull was clearly central to Bronze Age religion.) One, from Cnossus, dates from *c*.1500BC. Carved out of steatite with gilded horns, the bull's-head *rhyton* (ceremonial cup) has eyes of red jasper and white shell for the lines around its nostrils. It is a superb work by any standard but only 30cm (12in) high. Remarkably similar is the bull with golden horns and silver eyes found in a grave of Mycenae of about the same date.

The same style remained dominant on the mainland until the fall of Mycenaean civilization after 1200BC. How far Minoan and Mycenaean art survived or resurfaced to influence later Greek art is debatable. But the naturalism and humanism that distinguish it from grandiose contemporary art in Egypt or Babylon were also to be among the hallmarks of Hellenic art proper.

A distinctive Minoan sculpture emerged when the first palaces were built in Crete *c*.2000BC. Initially rather stiff, this had developed by *c*.1700BC into a lively and fluid art. It peaked around 1500BC just as Crete was devastated by the eruption of Thira, a blow from which it never fully recovered.

Sculptors made small figurines of bronze, clay or other materials (but seldom of marble) or in sculptured mouldings on murals and vases. Minoan artists never attempted the monumental.

ATHLETES AND GODDESSES

The Minoans and Mycenaeans anticipated later Greeks in the importance they attached to athletics, including – in Crete at least – the perilous sport of bull-leaping. A figurine from the palace at Cnossus of 1500BC of a young acrobat or bull-leaper caught in mid-air, carved in wood once covered with gold, reveals a classic naturalism. More of its time is the bronze votive figurine a mere 15cm (6in) high of *c*.1550BC. The slim young man, almost naked, has a markedly concave back, a Cretan ideal, and his right hand is raised to his forehead.

The deity he was worshipping may have been the Snake-Goddess, a frequent image in Minoan art. In a painted faience statue about 30cm (12in) high found in the temple depository of Cnossus, the goddess is shown dressed in the height of Minoan court fashion: long, flounced skirts, tight bodice with breasts exposed. The figure may, however, represent a priestess rather than the actual goddess.

Above: The Snake-Goddess, a typically colourful painted Minoan figurine, about 30cm (12in) high, of the 16th century BC. Some archaeologists now think this statue has been put together from disparate pieces.

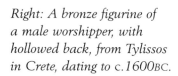

Right: A bronze figurine of a male worshipper, with hollowed back, from Tylissos in Crete, dating to c.1600BC.

Although few court ladies carried writhing snakes in each hand, as she does, sacred serpents were common in Minoan and later religion. (The goddess Athena was portrayed 1,000 years later in the Parthenon with a great snake coiling beside her. As there are references in the Linear B tablets at Cnossus to a goddess Athena, it is even possible that this image is of Athena.)

THE *LILY PRINCE*

An equally famous image of Minoan Crete is the *Lily Prince*, an unusually large-scale figure, about 2.1m (7ft) high on a relief fresco from Cnossus Palace. Heavily – and contentiously – restored, this graceful courtier or prince, almost naked apart from his kilt and feathered headdress, probably dates from *c.*1500BC. The figure embodies Cretan gracefulness, although he is unusually stiff.

By contrast, the *Harvester Vase* has vivid relief scenes of everyday rural life. It shows farmers laughing and chatting, presumably on the way back from harvest as they are carrying farming tools. The vase shows that Minoan artists were not interested only in courtiers.

A similarly vivid brilliant art in miniature appears in seals just 2.5cm (1in) in diameter from the mainland. One, probably dating to *c.*1300BC from a tomb near Sparta, shows a priest and a griffin, a mythical creature; another from the same tomb portrays two ducks with curved necks and is a triumph of Minoan or Mycenaean artistic naturalism.

THE LION GATE

Only one example of Mycenaean monumental sculpture survives: the great stone lions flanking the Lion Gate at Mycenae itself. Built *c.*1280BC, the Lion Gate consists of giant slabs of carved ashlar,

Right: The Lion Gate at Mycenae, dating from c.1280BC, *displays Mycenaean sculpture at its most powerful. But it is the only large-scale carving to survive from the Aegean Bronze Age.*

each weighing several tons. The now-lost heads of the two stone lions once snarled down in realistic fury. The sculpture's power may derive from Hattusa, the massively walled Hittite capital in Anatolia, but the lions flank a Minoan-style column. Sculptures would frequently be incorporated in temples by Classical Greeks, but the Lion Gate seems to have been a one-off in the Aegean Bronze Age.

Above: Tiny seals, often only 2.5cm (1in) long, reveal Mycenaean art at its vivid best. This seal, showing mythical beasts carrying offerings, dates from c.1300BC.

THE DARK AGES AND EARLY ARCHAIC PERIOD 1100–700BC

The collapse of Mycenaean civilization after 1200BC led to the Greek Dark Ages. Even less is known about this period than the Bronze Age, but artistically it certainly appears to deserve its name. The end of the elaborate palace-centred culture seemingly meant a nearly complete end to almost all artistic life for at least two centuries.

Only in Athens, safe thanks to its almost impregnably high rock and perhaps to its relative obscurity, did some form of civilized life in a sub-Mycenaean spirit continue without interruption. It was in Athens also that the first signs of a new art began to emerge. Such signs are, however, generally unimpressive before 800BC. During the 8th century BC the first truly Greek sculpture hesitantly takes shape, formed by the austere contemporary Geometric style that owed nothing to Bronze Age precedents.

STATUES FROM THE DIPLYON CEMETERY

Among the ivory figurines found in the Diplyon cemetery at Athens, one has a crown decorated with a meander pattern. This probably indicates that she is a goddess. Eastern influence underlies the choice of ivory as a raw material – there were never any elephants in Greece, so the material as well as the idea must have been imported – but there is a Greek solidity even in tiny figures only 24cm (9½in) tall. (Most items that have been recovered come from cemeteries or are votive offerings made to the gods.)

STATUES FROM OLYMPIA

From Olympia come several fine small bronzes of the mid-8th century BC. One shows a deer being attacked by dogs, another shows a man with a dog fighting a lion (this is a confused piece that takes some deciphering).

Above: This bronze figurine of a warrior in the Geometric style of the late 8th century BC heralds the revival of Greek sculpture after the Dark Ages. The naked human form was already the focus of interest.

Above: This head from the Diplyon cemetery at Athens reveals the highly stimulating impact of Asian art on Greek sculpture around 600BC.

Far more clearly depicted in action are the linked figurines of *The Hero and Centaur*, in which a man (or possibly a god, most probably Zeus) is shown with his arms locked around a centaur, a mythical beast shown as alternately wise and savage and long popular in Greek art. They are probably engaged in mortal combat.

Carved on a bronze tripod found at Olympia and dating from *c.*700BC, a vivid scene shows Apollo and Heracles fighting over a tripod. On a gentler note is a hind suckling her fawn.

More common than such bronze pieces as votive offerings – because they were far cheaper – are small terracotta figures

Above: Small, stiffly made bronze statues of animals dating from the late 8th century BC, the very dawn of Greek art proper.

such as that representing, rather than actually depicting, a horse of the late 8th century BC.

More realistic is the terracotta bird found in a cemetery south of the Eridanus in Athens. From such tiny, stiff, twig-like figurines, the whole grand tradition of Greek sculpture would develop.

BRONZE CASTING

Most of the greatest Greek statues were made in bronze, a material favoured because of its strength, durability and the way in which it can be easily worked.

Bronze is an alloy that typically consists of about 90 per cent copper, the rest being tin or other materials, including sometimes small amounts of lead or zinc. Bronze is easier to cast than copper because of its lower melting point. Its great tensile strength enables protruding parts – arms and legs – to be cast without supports, giving it an advantage over marble. Bronze statues' colour vary according to the amount of tin or other metals used, ranging from silverish to a rich red.

As it ages, bronze acquires a pleasing patina, although the Greeks painted all their bronze statues meticulously. Unfortunately, bronze has also always been highly valued as a metal, so most ancient statues were later melted down.

Initially, small bronze objects and tools were solid-cast in two-piece clay moulds. But by 1500BC larger statues were being

cast across the ancient world using the *cire perdue* (French: 'lost wax') method. In this type of casting, a clay core was formed in the basic shape of the statue. A thin layer of wax following the shape of the sculpture was encased within two layers of heat-resistant clay or plaster. As the wax heated up, it poured away. Wax gates let the wax out of the mould and the molten metal into the space that the 'lost wax' had created. Wax vents allowed hot gases to rise while the liquid bronze was being poured. As this cooled, it formed the statue. The master-mould could be reused many times.

The Riace bronzes of two warriors of *c.*460BC found in the sea near Reggio, Calabria in southern Italy, have almost identical bodies, although their heads are different. This suggests that their torsos were cast using the same mould, if perhaps at different times. Large-scale bronze statues were often cast in pieces no more than *c.*1m (3ft) long, for two men could only handle with ease a crucible containing *c.*9 litres (2 gallons) of molten bronze weighing *c.*68kg (150lb). Bronze must be poured quite fast or it will start to cool and not pour uniformly. If bronze is not at the right temperature to be sufficiently fluid, the casting may fail, resulting in the bronze cracking and becoming deformed as it cools.

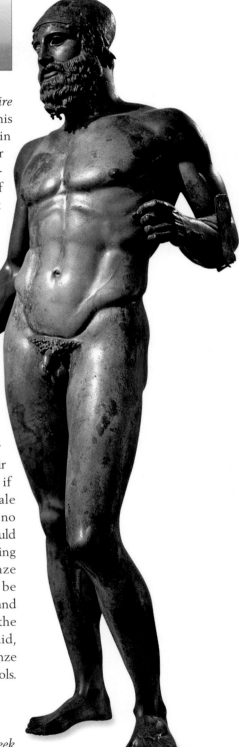

Right: One of the Riace bronzes, statues dating from c.460BC, in the Classical period, are among the masterpieces of Greek sculpture made possible by bronze casting.

THE IMPACT OF EGYPT
DAEDALIC SCULPTURE c.700–600BC

Egypt's pharaohs had successfully repelled the invasions of the 'Sea Peoples' that wrecked Bronze Age civilizations further north. Hardly affected by a dark age, this ancient, wealthy land continued to produce superb stone sculptures in its almost unchanging millennial tradition. In the early 7th century BC, as trade revived, the Greeks began retracing Mycenaean trade routes south to Egypt and east to the Levant. Soon Greeks were settling in Egypt as traders and mercenaries, causing friction with the Egyptians at times. Naucratis in the Delta was finally established as the sole Greek city in c.570BC.

The impact of Egyptian statues, monumental in every sense, was overwhelming on the simple Greeks of the Archaic Age (700–490BC). Egyptian sculpture, carved from stone, was designed to overawe, being hieratically stiff and often massive. Such hieratic grandeur inspired Greek artists to produce the sculptures called Daedalic, after the mythical Athenian artist who

had designed the Labyrinth for Minos in Crete. (If Daedalus had existed, he would of course have been a Mycenaean, but this distinction was unknown to later Greeks.) But Egypt's grand solemnity was balanced by colourful 'orientalizing' influences from Asia that often featured beasts, mythical or real.

BLOSSOMING OF ART

This fertilization led to a blossoming of Greek art from the mid-7th century BC. Among the first examples is the more than life-size statue of Artemis dedicated by Nikandre of Naxos. The goddess stands solidly imposing on her two long legs with arms flat at her side. The upper part of her body is emphasized, despite the smallness of her head, framed by the triangle of hair falling on her shoulders. The whole statue, with its unified balance of static form and dynamic force, exudes a tender calm. Smaller but equally impressive is the wooden statue of Hera from the great temple to that goddess in Samos of 650BC.

Of about the same date but in far better shape is the limestone *Auxerre Statuette*. She stands realistically, the curves of her skirt and half-naked breasts vividly carved, her long hair and facial features endowing her with feminine humanity. This statue proved influential across Greece, with similar statuettes being found at Rhodes, Corinth, Mycenae and Taranto, a colony in southern Italy.

The grandest sculptural achievement of the 7th century BC was the Lion Avenue of Delos. Nine seated lions flank the Sacred Way, each c.1.5m (5ft) high. The idea of such 'avenues' was Egyptian and they show Greek sculptors attempting, if not always achieving, monumentality. Of the gigantic statues cut from Cycladic marble quarries, some

Above: This kouros from Attica, made c.620BC, still displays marked Egyptian-inspired stiffness.

Below: The grandest sculptural achievement of the 7th century BC was the Lion Avenue of Delos. Nine seated lions flank the Sacred Way, each c.1.5m (5ft) high.

remained unfinished, clearly proving beyond their creators' powers. One such colossus that was abandoned half-hewn would have been 11m (36ft) high if it had been completed.

Lions were by then half-mythical creatures. They were probably extinct in Greece proper (though not in Macedonia), and so were treated fantastically, almost like sphinxes or chimaeras. From Corcyra (Corfu) in c.625BC comes a superb and quite realistic example. A mighty limestone lion, probably once part of a funerary monument, at 1.2m (4ft) long, lies menacingly on its plinth, its tail between its hind legs, forepaws extended, its fierce head expresses the dark menace of the wild.

KOUROS AND KOURE

But the focus of most Greek sculpture remained the human figure. Statues became increasingly impressive and large towards 620BC, as Greek sculptors gained confidence. The first great statues now emerge from Attica. The best-preserved is the *Kouros* by the 'Diplyon Master' of c.620BC. (Such naked archaic youths are called *kouros*, youth, and their female counterparts are called *koure*, maiden, the latter always portrayed fully clothed.)

Completely and proudly naked for the first time – unlike Egyptian statues – he stands more than lifesize at 1.84m (6ft 4in) tall, his long braided hair (an Archaic Greek fashion) well depicted. This kouros, imbued with Apollonian calm, probably stood on the grave of a young Athenian aristocrat, and embodies current ideals of beauty. Stylistic stiffness prevents complete realism, but anyway such statues were intended to represent, rather than depict accurately, human beings. The kouros remained a distinct type of statue down to 500BC, made according to specific rules.

A celebrated pair of kouroi are Cleobus and Biton by Polymedes of Argos of c.600 BC. They are bursting with muscular, youthful vigour. This is highly appropriate because, according to Herodotus the historian, these twin brothers pulled their mother in a heavy ox-cart to the Temple of Hera just in time for a ceremony, before sinking exhausted into a blessed oblivion granted to them by the gods as a reward.

Above: Found in Artemis' sanctuary on the island of Delos, with an inscription that it was dedicated to the goddess by Nikandre, this is the earliest extant all-marble statue. More than life-size, it dates to c.650BC.

Left: A celebrated pair of kouroi are Cleobus and Biton, probably made by Polymedes of Argos in c.600BC. They brim with muscular, youthful vigour.

THE 6TH-CENTURY AWAKENING c.600–490 BC

The whole tempo of Greek life – political, economic, intellectual and artistic – quickened in the 6th and early 5th centuries BC. In sculpture there was no sudden revolution or great leap forward comparable to that being made around the same time by philosophers in Ionia. Instead, there was a gradually accelerating discovery of naturalism that, with hindsight, paved the way for the titanic achievements in all the plastic arts of the next two centuries.

Slowly, the stiff geometry of an art inspired by Egypt, albeit less impressive, gave way to something more vivid and human and far more inspiring. What dominated Greek art at the time and for centuries afterwards was a persistent desire to express the ideal human form. Slow, unrecorded improvements in tools, running parallel with those in architecture, also gradually enabled sculptors to develop more expressive ways of carving.

THE ARCHAIC SMILE

Typical of statues of the beginning of the century is the sublimely calm, massive kouros from the shrine to Poseidon at Sunium. (The temple itself had not yet been built.) More than 3m (10ft) high, with a typically enigmatic, frozen Archaic smile, he was one of a pair of colossal figures visible from afar to seafarers. This recurrent Archaic smile was probably intended as a sign of a free citizen, for statues were still not intended actually to portray an individual. But names and inscriptions on the base begin to appear, making the kouroi more personal.

This is apparent in the koure (maiden) commemorating Phrasikleia, originally from Paros of c.550BC, which bears the rather cryptic dedication: "I could be called *koure* (maiden) for ever instead of wedded by the gods thus named, Ariston of Paros created me."

The so-called Apollo of Temea of around the same date was a funerary memorial statue, like many in the 6th century, almost life-size at 1.5m (5ft). He still has the fixed smile and elaborate long hair of the "young light-hearted masters of the waves" (Homer's phrase), but his body is treated more realistically

Above: This statue of Croesus, an Athenian killed fighting, dates from c.535BC. His muscles and bones are clearly modelled and his arms hang freely from his body.

Right: This sublimely calm, massive kouros, c.525BC, from the shrine to Poseidon at Sunium, is over 3m (10ft) high. With a typically fixed, enigmatic Archaic smile, he was probably one of two colossal figures.

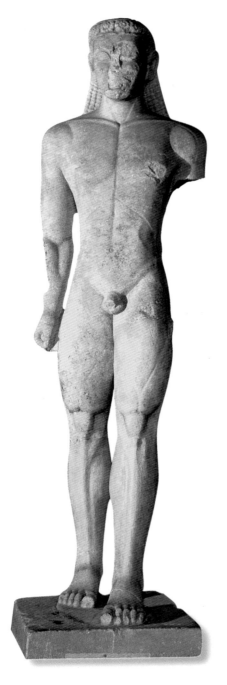

and smoothly. Slightly later, *c.*535BC, is the statue of Croesus, with the inscription: "Stand and grieve at the tomb of Croesus, killed in the front line by Ares (the war god)".

Croesus was a member of the powerful Alcmaeonid clan, enemies of Pisistratus who had become tyrant in 547BC. Croesus was presumably killed in internoble feuding. His muscles and bones are far more clearly modelled and his arms hang freely from his body. Even more realistic but badly damaged – giving it a

probably unjustly brutish air – is the statue marked on its base 'Aristodicus.' He has short hair – a sign of dawning Classicism – and a natural rather than pinched-in waist, but he retains a stiff Archaic pose.

TEMPLE SCULPTURE

Equally important were the sculptures adorning temples, now being built in increasing numbers. At the Treasury of the Siphnians in Delphi, a radically new marble temple built *c.*525BC, were placed not only the famous marble caryatids but also a fine frieze showing the Council of the Gods. Like all sculptures, in bronze or marble, it was originally painted. From the Acropolis in Athens several votive kouroi still depict the maidens with enigmatic fixed smiles and stiffly elaborate robes, indicting their noble pedigree, but the shape of their bodies starts to emerge, hinting at a new realism. These date from the late 6th century BC and, like most sculptures then on the Acropolis, were damaged or sullied during the Persian invasions of 480–479BC, so that they were later jettisoned. On the metopes of the great new temple of Aphaea on Aegina some carvings are Archaic, such as the man hurrying to help a fallen comrade, and others Classical. Classicism arrived with a rush.

ON THE CUSP OF CLASSICISM

Classicism can be seen emerging in one of the rare surviving early bronzes, the *Apollo of Piombino*. Dating from *c.*490BC and found off the coast of Italy, this retains the long hair and formulaic pose of an Archaic figure but has the fully muscled torso of a Classical statue. Generally similar and thought to date from *c.*480BC – on the brink of the Persian invasion – is the *Standing Youth*, a gigantic 1.9m (6ft 3in) bronze figure. His long hair again looks Archaic but his flowing sculptural forms also show Greek art on the cusp of Classicism. He may have been a young Apollo, for his left hand may have held the god's bow.

Above: The still half-Archaic figure of a moscophoros *(calf-carrier) dating from* c.580BC *has increasingly realistic muscles.*

Left: The Apollo of Piombino, *found in the sea off Italy and dating from* c.490BC, *has the long hair and stiff pose of Archaic figures but the muscled torso is that of Classical statues.*

THE DAWN OF CLASSICISM
c.480–450BC

Right: The bronze originals of these Roman marble copies were made in 477BC by Critios and Nesiotes, honouring the Athenian tyrannicides Harmodius and Aristogeiton. Both show for the first time the 'hardness' of early Classicism, with muscles emphasized.

Below: One of the two Riace bronzes, either athletes or warriors, depicted with unprecedented realism, made in c.470–460BC.

No earlier period in history matches the phenomenally rapid development of 5th-century BC Greece. After the Persians were defeated in 480–479BC, Athens became the pre-eminent Greek city, fully democratic. In high Classicism it realized its ideal style. In sculpture, the male nude was the focus of most attention, with female figures still being depicted fully clothed. Women were long considered of secondary interest in Greek art, as in Greek life.

REVOLUTIONARY REALISM

The *Critios Boy* of c.480BC (attributed to the sculptor Critios) is a standing youth wholly freed from the kouros conventions. He rests his weight realistically on his left leg, with his right leg slack, his right thigh pushed forward. His pelvis is correspondingly tilted, his right buttock slackened, his head and shoulders slightly inclined. This revolutionary realism comes closer to depicting a 'real' relaxed figure than any earlier artwork anywhere in the world. To create such a figure required genuine understanding of the human body. However the boy is also an idealized figure. For the first time the human body is depicted as perfectly beautiful and simultaneously symmetrical. Greek artists of the time were obsessed with mathematical symmetry. The statue is, however, atypical in one important way, for most Classical statues in the 5th century BC were in bronze, not marble. Sculptors now began to think in terms of 'moulding' – for bronze

casting – rather than 'carving', even when they were actually working in marble, as in this instance.

THE RIACE BRONZES

This sculptural concern is evident in the magnificent Riace bronzes, fished from the sea near Riace in southern Italy in 1972. Dating from c.470–460BC, these two athletes or warriors have vigorous muscular bodies, depicted realistically. Their resting limbs convey the tension of recent exertions superbly. Each torso is nearly a mirror image of the other, conceivably cast from the same mould. Only their heads truly differ. They retain traces of copper on their lips and nipples, silver on their teeth and precious stones in their eyes. They were perhaps part of a group, among the many superb Greek artworks that the Romans looted. However, they are probably not by Pheidias, the great Athenian sculptor as was at one time thought, for they are not in his serenely idealizing style and are a little too early.

THE CHARIOTEER

A noble example of very early Classicism, in which traces of the Archaic style linger, is the *Delphi Charioteer*. Probably presented by Hieron, tyrant of Syracuse, as a votive offering after his victory at Cumae over the Etruscans and datable to *c*.473BC, the young charioteer has a solemnity suited to Greece's holiest shrine. He originally stood in the car of a four-horse bronze chariot with a groom standing beside him. Only this statue of the group has survived, thanks to an earthquake that dropped him down a

Below: The Delphi Charioteer *is a superb example of early Classicism, probably presented by Hieron, tyrant of Syracuse, as a votive offering after his victory at Cumae, so datable to* c.473BC.

ravine into an old drain. There he was somehow overlooked by subsequent pillagers of the shrine.

The extreme verticality of the statue would not have been so marked when he was riding inside his chariot. He wears the long robes suited to his windy profession, with a diadem band around his head. His eyes are marked in coloured stones and traces remain of the gilt once on his hair, eyes and lips. This must have given his face a richness and living warmth typical of Greek statues but hard to imagine today when looking at chilly marble copies.

THE TYRANNICIDES

In Athens itself two statues made at around this time commemorate what might be called Athens' first freedom fighters: Harmodius and Aristogeiton. These famed 'tyrannicides' were two (male) lovers who killed the tyrant Hipparchus in 514BC. They did so out of sexual jealousy but in so doing unwittingly paved the way for Athens' democratic revolution soon after – hence their statues prominently placed on the Acropolis. The first statues, possibly made by Antenor who had worked at Delphi, were carried off by King Xerxes to Persepolis when he sacked Athens in 480BC. Their replacements, the bronze originals of these Roman marble copies, were made in 477BC by Critios and Nesiotes. (Alexander the Great later returned the originals when he in turn burnt Persepolis in 330BC, but they have since vanished.)

These figures may be only Roman copies, but their heroic, masculine figures incarnate determined political action. The onlooker is effectively in the position of their victim. Slightly larger than life at 1.93m (6ft 4in), they reveal for almost the first time the notable 'hardness' of the Early Classical style, with their side muscles above their thighs emphasized unrealistically to increase the impression of male strength.

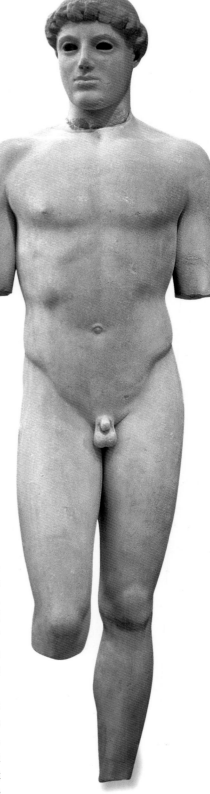

Above: The Critios Boy *of* c.480BC, *the work that marks the sudden arrival of Classicism, is at once naturalistic and idealized.*

IMAGES OF THE GODS

Above: Apollo, the archetypal Hellenic god of order, reason and light, carved on the western pediment of the Temple of Zeus at Olympia, 5th century BC. He is portrayed as a calm and pitiless deity, supremely confident in his inhuman beauty and power.

The portrayal of the gods as supremely perfect but utterly realistic human beings – the greatest achievement of Classicism – was perfected in the middle decades of the 5th century BC. From the sea off Artemisium on the island of Euboea comes one magnificent bronze. (Bronze does not rust in seawater, so shipwrecks have paradoxically proved excellent at preserving such works.) Once thought to be a statue of the sea-god Poseidon wielding a triton since lost, he is now considered to represent Zeus, king of the gods, hurtling his divine thunderbolt at an unseen adversary.

A NAMELESS MASTERPIECE

This Zeus is the work of an unknown master who clearly was a genius, not just a talented local carver. The figure probably originated in northern Greece and was being transported south, perhaps like many Greek artworks to a Roman customer, when it was shipwrecked. (If it had been travelling north, it might have been the work of Onatas of Aegina.) While attempts to identify this masterpiece with a specific statue mentioned in literary sources have failed, it is securely dated on stylistic grounds to *c.*460BC, as Classicism was approaching its peak.

Certainly Zeus' features have the Homeric majesty expected of the king of Olympus and lord of thunder. Standing more than lifesize at 2.1m (6ft 10in), as befits a god, he is complete apart from his eyes, which were once inlaid with coloured stones. His hair is tied back by a braid, usual for the time, but otherwise he is shown sublimely naked, humanity raised to divine levels. His body is powerful but not absurdly muscular. His arms are unrealistically long, but presumably this was a deliberate stylization. He is the noblest Classical bronze statue of a god to survive.

THE TEMPLE OF ZEUS AT OLYMPIA

But the chief centre of sculptural activity in Greece during the second quarter of the 5th century was at Olympia, site of the Olympic Games, a shrine second only to Delphi in Panhellenic importance. Here, in the sacred precinct around the great Temple to Zeus built in the 460s BC stood literally hundreds of statues of victors in the games. For competitors were taking part in a sacred rite, not just competing for a prize. Religion permeated athletics as it did almost every aspect of Greek life.

Unfortunately Christianity, a later religion, so detested such statues that only their bases remain. Some bronzes were

Left: One of the 12 metopes from the great Temple of Zeus at Olympia depicting the 11th labour of Hercules, carved by the anonymous 'Master of Olympia' in c.460BC.

destroyed on the orders of the emperor Theodosius I, a Christian zealot, when the Games were suppressed in c.AD393; others were looted or melted down for their valuable metal. The Temple to Zeus, only destroyed finally by an earthquake in the 6th century AD, was richly decorated with stone sculptures on its metopes. These have been pieced together to give a good idea of the work sometimes attributed to the 'Master of Olympia', an unknown sculptor (or sculptors) of undoubted genius, working in the severe style of early Classicism.

THE TWELVE LABOURS OF HERCULES

Hercules (Heracles) was the archetypal Greek mythical hero, semi-divine as a son of Zeus, and seen as the personification of physical strength and *areté* (excellence). Hercules was credited with founding the Olympic Games. To expiate the sin of killing his own family in a fit of madness, Hercules was ordered to carry out 12 almost impossible 'labours'. The 12 metopes of the Temple of Zeus at Olympia illustrate these in the 'severe' style, with figures about one and a half times life-size.

Among the best preserved is the 11th labour, Hercules' mission to fetch the golden apples of the Hesperides, the islands of the Blessed. Hercules passed on this particular labour to the giant Atlas, offering to carry the burden of the heavens on his own shoulders meanwhile. Atlas is shown returning with the apples in his hands to Hercules, who stands with every muscle in his body taut, upholding his titanic burden. Although the goddess

Right: The majestic face of Zeus, king of the gods, as portrayed by an unknown sculptor who was clearly a genius. Recovered from the sea off Artemisium, the Zeus is dated on stylistic grounds to c.460BC.

Athena, Hercules' helper in his trials, is putting a cushion on his shoulder to reduce the strain, the impression of tortured strength is overwhelming. Yet the hero's body is not that of some grotesquely over-muscled bodybuilder but harmoniously symmetrical.

APOLLONIAN SERENITY

One of the finest images of Apollo, the archetypal god of reason, comes from the west pediment of the Temple of Zeus. Apollo is shown, right arm raised in serene authority, quelling the bestial fury of the drunken centaurs. Calm, pitiless, supremely confident in his physical beauty, he is untroubled by any doubt or compassion. Hercules' body is relatively flat and inexpressive compared to some contemporary works, but this only increases his divine yet dangerous power. Dating from c.450BC, this statue is the only original large-scale Apollo of the Early Classical Age that has survived intact.

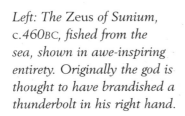

Left: The Zeus of Sunium, c.460BC, fished from the sea, shown in awe-inspiring entirety. Originally the god is thought to have brandished a thunderbolt in his right hand.

PHEIDIAS, MAKER OF THE GODS ACTIVE C.460–430BC

Above: A model of the giant statue of Athena Parthenos, *made by Pheidias in c.438BC in chryselephantine for the interior of the new Parthenon.*

Considered by many the greatest Classical sculptor, Pheidias (*c.*490–*c.*428BC) was an Athenian citizen and a close friend of Pericles, the supreme democratic statesman. Little is known of his life, although he reputedly studied under Hegias. By 447BC he had become effectively Athens' Minister for the Arts as he oversaw the building of the Parthenon, that pinnacle of Greek architecture and sculpture.

Pheidias created idealized forms so realistic yet sublime that he was called 'Maker of the gods'. Infuriatingly, not one freestanding work by him survives and Roman copies are even feebler than normal. However, we have many of the superb Parthenon carvings, including the Elgin Marbles now in the British Museum. This project, far too large for one man to execute, required scores of skilled sculptors, most working to Pheidias' designs and under his supervision. Carved in high relief, many figures are depicted almost in the round, leaping from their frames with remarkable vigour.

IMAGES OF ATHENA
Pheidias was most famous for his giant statues of gods. The first was *Athena Lemnia* (made for colonists of Lemnos) of 450BC, still partly in the 'severe' style. More typical was the huge statue *Athena Parthenos* (Virgin) that Pheidias made for the new Parthenon's interior, completed in 438BC. Standing *c.*12m (40ft) high, she was of chryselephantine: her skin was covered in ivory and her robes and armour in gold, fitted over a wooden core. She carried a winged Nike in her right hand. A shield rested on the ground

Left: The Apollo of the Tiber, *a Roman copy of a bronze original from Pheidias' workshop, perhaps by the master himself, suggests something of Pheidias' idealized but monumental style.*

to her left, while a huge serpent coiled beside her. On her head was a triple-crested helmet. A pool of water in front reflected a dim sacred light on to this opulent cult image.

Outside on the Acropolis, Pheidias created another, more militant, image of the goddess *Athena Promachos* (Warrior) in bronze with shield, helmet and gilded spear, standing inside the Propylaea and immediately obvious to worshippers. The goddess was also visible far out to sea, proclaiming Athens' power and glory.

THE PARTHENON CARVINGS
The frieze running around the Parthenon, started in 447BC, is 60m (175 yards) long. More of it has survived in reasonable condition than any other sculpture of the age. However, it must have been hard to see many figures easily when *in situ*. Some may be by Pheidias himself: all reveal his spirit. The riders shown on the west frieze, young cavaliers naked apart from their cloaks, are taking part in the four-yearly Panathenaic Procession, the greatest event in Athens' civic and religious calendar. On the east frieze graceful, noble-looking gods and heroes process, also part of the festival. In thus worshipping its patron goddess, Athens also worshipped its idealized self.

Fine examples of *centauromachia* (centaur battles) from the temple's south side have been read as depicting Athenian civilization triumphing over savagery. But the centauromachia was always a popular theme, for it allowed sculptors to depict man and beast in combat. The west pediment showed Poseidon and Athena fighting for the city's loyalty – a contest Athena won by her gift of an olive tree. This central section has been lost but from the east pediment a masterly realistic study shows the wine-god Dionysus reclining wholly naked. Aphrodite,

goddess of love, is also reclining but with arched, quivering body. While she is fully clothed, her clinging dress reveals more than it conceals of her beauty.

WONDER OF THE WORLD

Pheidias, unjustly accused of embezzlement by Pericles' enemies, left Athens in 432BC for Olympia. Ancient writers considered the giant statue of Zeus he made there for the Temple of Zeus in c.430BC his masterpiece. It later ranked as one of the Seven Wonders of the World. Zeus was shown on a high throne, holding a Nike in his right hand and sceptre in his left. This was also a chryselephantine statue. Although portrayed seated, at seven times life size, 13m (42ft) high, Zeus almost touched the temple's ceiling. Only coins give us any idea of this work.

One statue survives to convey something of Pheidias' monumental style: the *Apollo of the Tiber*, a Roman copy of a bronze Apollo, perhaps by the master himself. The tall, graceful god looks down

Right: A Lapith and centaur fighting, from the Parthenon's south side, a contest at times read as depicting Athens' triumphing over barbarism, carved to Pheidias' designs.

with serene, dreamy detachment. This work and the Parthenon sculptures epitomize Pheidias' High Classicism. In it the human body, perfectly understood from within, is portrayed with an idealized yet wholly naturalistic harmony.

Above: A detail of the Elgin Marbles, from the west frieze of the Parthenon showing horsemen in the Panathenaic Procession, carved to Pheidias' designs in c.440BC.

POLYCLITUS AND MYRON
ACTIVE 460–420 BC

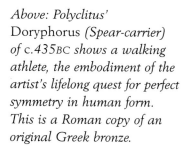

Polyclitus, a rival of Pheidias, pursued a very different approach to Classicism. Coming from Argos, he worked at times in Athens. One of the great intellectuals of Greek art, Polyclitus declared: "A well-made work results from numerous calculations, executed to within a hair's breadth." His statues did not aim to please but to incarnate the principles of mathematical beauty he had outlined in his book *The Canon*. This has not survived, nor have his original bronzes. He may have worked exclusively in bronze but we have only blockish marble copies that distort his genius. Only one marble copy, the *Theseus Diadoumenus*, is truly impressive.

SYMMETRICAL SOLIDITY
Polyclitus sought not to depict an idealized realism but to fulfil his quest for depicting symmetry in the human form. He succeeded triumphantly with the *Doryphorus* (Spear-carrier) of *c.*435 BC. This shows a walking athlete/hero (he probably once held a spear). The weight of his body rests on one foot, his relaxed left leg bears no weight, his right hand hangs down freely. The sloping line of his hips resulting from his pose is carried through the torso into a correspondingly opposed shoulder line later called *contrapposto*. All his body is drawn into this movement but his torso itself is stockily solid, with the typically heavily emphasized muscles.

Polyclitus' work was much admired and copied in antiquity. A true idea of his genius emerges in the *Torso of Doryphorus*, a copy in polished basalt that resembles bronze far more closely than marble. The *Prima Porta* statue of Augustus 400 years later repeated the *Doryphorus*'s stance, although the emperor is clothed. So did images of the body-builder Charles Atlas in the 20th century.

Above: Polyclitus' Doryphorus *(Spear-carrier) of* c.435 BC *shows a walking athlete, the embodiment of the artist's lifelong quest for perfect symmetry in human form. This is a Roman copy of an original Greek bronze.*

Right: The symmetrical solidity typical of Polyclitus' work marks this statue, which once again is a Roman marble copy of an original Greek bronze.

THESEUS DIADOUMENUS
This statue shows the legendary Athenian king as a victorious young athlete crowned with a diadem. The body is still solidly muscular but the youth's face reveals a softer side to Polyclitus' puritanical art, being delicately carved. Polyclitus also sculpted an Amazon, winning a competition at Ephesus with it. His wounded Amazon, shown bare-breasted, is leaning against a post, the first

time that a figure was shown supporting itself against another object. While still more athletic than feminine in form, she reveals the sculptor's versatility. Polyclitus is credited with making the great statue of the goddess Hera in Argos, which some writers preferred to Pheidias' statue of *Zeus* at Olympia.

MYRON ACTIVE 450–430BC

The third great sculptor of the 5th century, Myron, tended to an extreme realism. This was evident in his bronze cow on the Acropolis, said to be real enough to be mistaken for actual flesh and bones. (It was of course painted.) This statue has vanished, as has his renowned statue, the *Discobolus* (discus thrower). Lucian, a writer of the 2nd century AD, describes the original as "stooping in the pose of a man preparing to throw, turning towards the hand with the discus and gently bending the knee, as ready to rise and throw." Numerous marble copies of this work exist, showing the swing of the taut, muscular body. It looks so realistic some athletes have tried to emulate it – in vain, for this is no snapshot. The support behind the *Discobolus* was needed for

marble copies but not the bronze original. (Hitler so admired a copy of this work in Rome that he persuaded Mussolini to send it to Germany. It was returned to Italy after 1945.)

Myron was also famous for his bronze *Athena and Marsyas*. This does not survive as a group even in marble copies but has been reconstructed. According to Pausanias in the 2nd century AD, it showed "Athena striking Marsyas Silenus for taking up the flute that the goddess wished thrown away". Marsyas was a satyr, one of the licentious half-goats, over-proud of his flute-playing. Athena. who disdained such vulgar music-making because it distorted the face, clutches her spear, the model of Olympian calm, looking down at the satyr. Marsyas met a ghastly end: he competed on his pipe with Apollo, lost and was then flayed alive as a punishment.

Above: A Roman copy of a part of the bronze original of Athena and Marsyas by Myron.

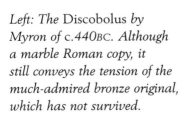

Left: The Discobolus *by Myron of* c.440BC. *Although a marble Roman copy, it still conveys the tension of the much-admired bronze original, which has not survived.*

UNVEILING APHRODITE
*c.*420–390BC

Above: Paionius of Mende made this magnificent winged Nike (Victory), *which was dedicated at Olympia by the Messenians in 421BC.*

While the male nude fascinated the greatest sculptors of the 5th century BC, the female nude was for long almost ignored. There was one exception: the *Esquiline Venus*, a marble copy of a bronze statue, showing a short but sensual figure, very realistic and completely naked, of *c.*450BC. But she was seemingly a one-off. This ignoring in part rose from the notoriously low status of women in Classical Athens. Their restricted appearance in art also reflected the tastes of a tough, heroic age, when sculptors found the muscular angularity of the male body, toned by constant exercise, more artistically challenging than the female body's curves.

By the last decades of the century, however, as the increasingly catastrophic Peloponnesian War ground on, tastes began to change. A less heroic, more sensually delighting art became appreciated

and the female form acquired – or regained – its fundamental appeal for sculptors, an appeal never since lost.

For a long time the female body was shown only under drapery. Increasingly, however, this consisted of thin clinging robes that gave almost a 'wet look'. This emphasized rather than concealed the body, until finally the female form emerged wholly naked.

THE WINGED GODDESS

The first half of the Peloponnesian War went relatively well for Athens and her allies, which included those Messenians not enslaved by Sparta. The Messenians, to commemorate their part in the victory over the Spartans at Sphacteria in 425BC, dedicated a statue of Nike at Olympia in *c.*421BC, with the inscription: "The Messenians and Naupactians dedicate her

Right: Nike Unlacing her Sandal, *from the Temple of Athena Nike on the Acropolis of* c.420BC.

GRAVE STONES

In sober contrast to such increasingly sensual statues are the tomb reliefs, particularly common in the later stages of the Peloponnesian War as Athenian casualties mounted. (Tombstones, while often found in the Archaic period, were for some reason rare in the early 5th century BC.) These usually took an architectural form with a pediment, as if the figures were outside the door of a home. Domesticity is the keynote, a reminder that even Athenians at their most public-spirited had their own families, which were the acknowledged foundation of society. The tomb of Hegeso and her servant commemorates the dead Hegeso, shown choosing a piece of jewellery from a box held by her maid. Even in this funereal carving of *c.*410BC, Hegeso's clothing reveals her body remarkably clearly.

Above: The tomb of Hegeso and her servant, commemorating a citizen's dead wife. Even in this funereal carving of c.410BC, Hegeso's light clothing reveals her body clearly.

to the Olympian Zeus as a tithe of the enemy's booty. Paionius of Mende made her." Mende was in northern Greece but Paionius worked mostly in Olympia, where he made this statue, an original work in marble, one of the masterpieces of Greek art.

Nike, winged goddess of victory, is shown at the moment of alighting to crown success on the battlefield. The wind of her flight bares one breast and presses her clothing close against her wonderfully lithe body, some 2.2m (7ft) high. Paionius has managed to convey motion at the point of being arrested with brilliant vividness. There was originally an eagle, emblem of Zeus, at her feet, and she stood on a pillar about 10m (33ft) high. Unusually at the time, Paionius signed the work on the dedication block, a sign of his pride in his achievement.

NIKE UNLACING HER SANDAL
Work on the smaller temples of the Athenian Acropolis continued despite the wars that stopped in 421BC only to restart in 415BC. Smallest and most exquisite of the temples overlooking the city was that of Athena Nike (Athena as Victory) built by Mnesicles about 428–423BC. Its frieze, which probably dates from after 420BC, shows a series of divine or mythical figures engaged in vigorous yet oddly elegant combat. One of them soon became justly famous and much copied in antiquity, that of *Nike Unlacing her Sandal*, which flanked a small staircase at the west of the temple.

For once we have the original, if without her head. Her clinging drapery, brilliantly carved, reveals a lithe but very feminine body as she bends in a marvellously fluid movement to lace up her sandal. With her breasts half-revealed, her thighs pushing against the soft fabric, this conveys as much sensuality as a nude.

APHRODITE IN THE AGORA
The true goddess of love, however, was Aphrodite (Venus), not chaste Athena or militant Nike. Aphrodite could more easily be found in the Agora, the buzzing commercial and social heart of Athens, than on the heights of the Acropolis.

One statue of Aphrodite – which suffered the indignity of being used as filling in a late Roman wall, erected in panic against renewed invasions in the 3rd century AD – reveals an almost baroque touch in her swirling robes that could slip off her at any moment. She could just be the work of Callimachus, who was one of the most famous sculptors of the late 5th century BC, although no works firmly attributed to him have survived. Callimachus was renowned for his free-flowing but fastidious grace, casting bronze 'like lace' – although some found his skills excessively ornate. He also reputedly pioneered the use of the drill in sculpture.

Below: The Esquiline Venus, *a marble copy of a bronze of c.450BC by an unknown artist, may be the first female nude in Greek art. Although not typically idealized, she emanates a gentle sensuality.*

THE 4TH-CENTURY BC REVOLUTION

Above: A marble relief copy of Timotheus' lost bronze masterpiece, Leda and the Swan. *This illustrates the myth in which Zeus, assuming a swan's form, seduced Leda, depicted here with novel sympathy and tenderness.*

The Peloponnesian War ended in 404BC with Athens' total defeat. Sparta took over Athens' empire and proceeded to misgovern it, so causing resentment and further wars. These proved inconclusive, exhausting and disillusioning. Although Athenian democracy was restored after a short-lived fascist junta and democracy even spread to other cities such as Thebes later, the *polis* (the 'citizen-state') no longer commanded the same passionate undivided loyalty from its citizens that it had. Instead, private life – or life in the secluded grounds of an Academy like Plato's founded just outside the walls of Athens – proved increasingly attractive. This retreat from the public sphere, although by no means complete, gathered pace after Alexander the Great's conquests opened up a vast new world. They made life in the old polis seem less wholly satisfying to many people.

THE TOMBSTONE OF DEXILEUS
This mood was reflected in art, as the idealized, heroic but impersonal high Classicism of the previous century gave way to a new individualism. The new era's artists discovered people's real personalities, shown by their backgrounds and deeds. The art of truly individual portraiture emerged hesitantly.

An early example of this is the Tombstone of Dexileus of Thoricus, a young Athenian killed in the Battle of Corinth in 394BC. He is shown in the act of killing his crouching enemy. His pose on the rearing horse recalls the horsemen sculpted on the Parthenon 40 years before, but he seems oddly detached from the action, rather than heroically engaged. This is fitting for what was a private tombstone rather than a public monument.

Artists also began to discover women's personalities, just as they began to depict the female nude. Although in the male-dominated world of ancient Greece the female nude was never treated as frequently as the male (in contrast to the situation today), fully naked female statues now began to engage the greatest sculptors' attention. The finest sculptors were not concerned solely with depicting their bodies but developed new ways of portraying feminine emotions.

TIMOTHEUS AT EPIDAURUS
Timotheus (active 380–340BC) may have come from Epidaurus in north-eastern Peloponnese. He is recorded as being paid 500 drachmae for work on the sculptures of the pediment of its renowned Temple of Asclepius, the healer-god, in the early 4th century BC. However, he went on to work

Left: Timotheus made some of the carvings for the immense tomb of Mausolus, ruler of Halicarnassus, around 350BC – works of dynamic drama.

in several other cities, including Halicarnassus (now Bodrum in Turkey), where he made some of the dramatic carvings on the immense tomb for its dynast Mausolus.

From the acroteria of the Epidaurus temple a *Nike* by him survives. Although now only a battered fragment, it still reveals his remarkable talent in the way her right wing is raised to catch an invisible wind. Also from the temple is the almost intact figure of Hygeia, goddess of the hearth, another half-naked figure bending gracefully. (Other more complete figures such as Aura, a deity seemingly riding side-saddle, were probably executed by Theodotus, otherwise unknown, to Timotheus' designs.)

Timotheus was also responsible for the pediments of the temple. These have not survived but it is possible to reconstruct them. The west pediment depicted the Sack of Troy. This was hardly an original subject but one that Timotheus portrayed in a highly original manner by dwelling on the sufferings of the women in the captured city.

On the right side of the pediment a female figure, possibly Hecabe, King Priam's wife, turns to help her fatally wounded son, holding him in her arms as he collapses. The sorrows of other Trojan women such as Cassandra, about to be abducted, raped or killed by the victorious Achaeans, are also movingly depicted for almost the first time in Greek art.

LEDA AND THE SWAN
The masterpiece of Timotheus' maturity is his *Leda and the Swan*, a bronze that has since been lost. However, numerous marble copies survive, most of which are approximately life-size and give a good impression of the famous original. The work illustrates the myth in which Zeus, king of the gods, assumed a swan's shape to seduce Leda. She later gave birth to the divine twins Castor and Pollux. In the myth, Zeus also sent an eagle – not sculpted – which appeared to threaten the swan, a wily tactic that persuaded the

reluctant Leda to shelter the swan. Leda is shown holding her cloak up to hide the swan nestling against her, as she cranes her head anxiously upward. Her expression conveys mingled anxiety and innocence. No earlier Greek artist had ever managed to capture female emotions so convincingly.

In an *Athena* (another bronze, which is only known in marble copies), the imposing grandeur of the goddess as depicted by Pheidias has given way to a more girlish figure, which is far less exalted and godlike.

Above: The Tombstone of Dexileus, a young Athenian who died at the Battle of Corinth in 394BC. Shown killing his cowering enemy, he lacks the aloof heroism of 5th-century horsemen, partly because this is a private memorial, partly because the exhausted post-war age felt differently about war.

PRAXITELES
ARTIST OF THE CENTURY

Above: Praxiteles' Aphrodite of Cnidus *of* c.350BC, *"the finest statue in the world" according to Pliny.*

Praxiteles was ranked alongside Polyclitus, Pheidias and Lysippus by ancient writers as one of the supreme master sculptors. Working throughout the middle of the 4th century BC, he was renowned for the sensuous charm and grace of his art. This marked a further stage in the move away from the lofty idealism of high Classicism. Praxiteles was more concerned with portraying human emotions and creating gently beautiful objects, most famously his *Aphrodite of Cnidus*.

The master of sensual sweetness came from a family of sculptors. His father was the successful Athenian sculptor Cephisodotus, whose *Eirene* (peace) *Holding the Infant Ploutos* (wealth) was placed in the Athenian Agora in *c.*380BC. Such a prominent place for such a subject – inconceivable in earlier centuries – was a sign of the increasingly war-weary times. Praxiteles himself responded to the new mood by creating works of deliberate beauty, which may strike modern eyes as too smooth, bland and sugary. But if they fail to stir our emotions, they proved hugely influential then and long after. His son continued the family tradition after him in the same style.

APOLLO AND THE LIZARD
One of Praxiteles' earliest works to show his distinctive genius is his *Satyr Pouring Wine* of *c.*375BC. Although we have only marble copies of this bronze, they show already the artist's hallmark of charm and beauty in this graceful youth – no trace of the bestial satyr here. (The jug and his left forearm have not survived.) Even more graceful is the later *Apollo Sauroctamus* (*Apollo Playing with a Lizard*). This shows the god as a

Left: A satyr, leaning against a tree trunk, displays to the full Praxiteles' typically languid sensuality.

Above: Despite the ravages of time that have broken her nose, this Aphrodite, carved in Praxiteles' workshop in c.325BC, *has the soft beauty found in all his female figures.*

smooth-limbed, beardless boy teasing a lizard crawling up a tree trunk. Instead of the sublime grandeur of earlier statues of the god, here we see the deity enjoying a languid, blissful sensuality – another key aspect of the divine from now on, but one seldom recognized earlier.

A SURVIVING MASTERPIECE
In 1877 archaeologists at Olympia discovered a marble statue of *Hermes and the Infant Dionysus* in the exact location noted by Pausanias 1,700 years earlier. This is almost certainly the famed original by Praxiteles, who often worked in marble. (His preference for doing so helped make the material fashionable again after long neglect.)

Despite being savagely over-cleaned by enthusiastic restorers, the statue still conveys an immediate sense of the splendour and glory Praxiteles could create in marble. Hermes, the messenger-god, props the tiny Dionysus, the wine god and his half-brother, on a tree-trunk to play with the child and offer him a bunch of grapes (missing from the original). Hermes was escorting the orphaned baby to Mt Nysa to be looked after by nymphs. The group shows a novel tenderness among the gods. They are still perfectly formed beings but they now exhibit less crushingly Olympian emotions.

The work was probably made around 330BC. At 2.15m (7ft 2in), it is rather larger than lifesize.

"THE FINEST STATUE IN THE WHOLE WORLD"

Praxiteles' most original and acclaimed statue was his *Aphrodite*, again made in marble. This, the first full-scale totally naked female nude of the goddess of love, was ordered in *c*.350BC by the island of Cos. The islanders were so shocked by the goddess's unprecedented nudity that they refused it. The people of nearby Cnidus happily took it instead and it became one of the most admired artworks in the ancient world. People made long journeys just to see her. One man reputedly fell in love with her. He embraced her so passionately that he could only be prised off with difficulty and left an indelible mark on her surface. Later, Pliny the Elder, the Roman writer of the 1st century AD, called her "the finest statue not just by Praxiteles but in the whole world".

Again, we have only semi-competent later copies, but they still reveal Praxiteles' great originality. *Aphrodite*, at 2m (6ft 7in) more than life-size, is depicted as a mature, shapely woman who has probably just emerged from her bath. A towel or robe is draped over a nearby vase. Her right hand covers her private parts but the rest of her body is fully exposed to the view for the first time in Greek art. She is realistically proportioned, with her hips larger than her breasts. (Ancient Greek artists were never fixated on outsized breasts.)

The copies we have, though imperfect, are often complete. They have helped create an archetype of female beauty that would later inspire Renaissance artists such as Botticelli, Raphael, Titian and Veronese, and so much of subsequent Western art. Such accepted ideals of female beauty are still apparent in almost every magazine, advertisement and film that we see today.

Above: Apollo Sauroctamus, one of Praxiteles' masterpieces, shows the god as a smooth-limbed, beardless adolescent teasing a lizard on a tree trunk. Instead of the divine sublimity conveyed by earlier statues, Apollo is shown as sensually relaxed.

Left: Discovered at Olympia in 1877, this original marble shows Praxiteles' genius at its height. Hermes, the messenger god, props the tiny Dionysus, the wine-god, and also his half-brother, on a tree-trunk to play with the child, offering him a bunch of grapes.

SCOPAS
SCULPTOR OF ECSTASY

Above: The head of a warrior, attributed to Scopas or his school, with all the master's characteristic passion still evident despite its much-battered state.

Not all art in the 4th century BC depicted the idyllic joys of gods or nymphs in Arcadia. Scopas, who worked in the middle of the century, specialized in depicting human or divine passions at their most intense. Born on the island of Paros, noted for its marble quarries, he had a famously fiery temperament. This comes through in his art, which differs radically from that of his contemporary Praxiteles, although both men preferred marble to bronze.

Scopas is recorded as working on the Mausoleum of Halicarnassus, the biggest project of the time; the great Temple of Artemis at Ephesus (then being again rebuilt); and at the Temple of Athena at Tegea in the Peloponnese. According to Pausanias, he designed this last temple.

FRENZIED BACCHANTES
The sculptures decorating the Mausoleum at Halicarnassus, later declared one of the Seven Wonders of the World, took many years of effort by some of Greece's greatest living sculptors, including Timotheus, Leochares and Scopas. Scopas, according to Pliny the Elder, the encyclopaedic Roman commentator writing 400 years later, carved the reliefs on the huge pyramidical structure's east face. Most notable were his depictions of ecstatic women, especially

Maenads or Bacchantes. (These were the female followers of the wine-god Dionysus, liberated from the normal constraints on Greek women by the ambiguously beautiful god.)

Although no originals survive of Scopas' *Maenads*, an unusually fine Roman copy in Parian marble powerfully conveys the divine madness and unleashed energy of Scopas' work. The orgiastic Maenad, with her long flowing hair and shapely body, is simultaneously a beautiful young woman and the terrifying embodiment of daemonic ecstasy. "Who carved this Bacchante?" asked an epigram of the time. "Scopas." "Who filled her with wild delirium – Dionysus or Scopas?" "Scopas." Almost naked – her short robe accentuates rather than hides her thrusting, twisting body – she is caught up in the drama of the god of wine and ecstasy.

Another less violent but equally ecstatic figure, this time totally naked, is Scopas' *Tritoness* (*Sea Goddess*), known in a copy found at Ostia. Her head is thrown back in ecstasy, her long thick hair cascades over her shoulders and toward her breasts, her flesh is modelled with remarkable vividness. Such art – "that has brought to its aid the impulse of growing life itself, so unbelievable is what you see, so invisible is what you believe", in the words of Callistratus, a near-contemporary writer – was unprecedented in Greece, probably the whole world.

AMAZONS AND HEROES

Scopas' talent for depicting emotional extremes was not restricted to Bacchantes, however. The *Amazonomachia* (*Amazon Battle*), a fragment from some part of the

Left: The Amazonomachia *(Amazon Battle), a fragment from the Mausoleum at Halicarnassus attributed to Scopas. Unarmoured in their short tunics, the Amazons show themselves equal adversaries of the male warriors. Here, Scopas ignores all Classical restraint while still working fluently in the Classical idiom.*

Mausoleum at Halicarnassus that is attributed to Scopas, shows his skills in a more military field. The fighting swirls between the helmeted warriors with their shields and helmets and the acrobatic, almost airborne Amazons. Although defenceless in their short tunics, the Amazons demonstrate that they are very much the warriors' equals. Their portrayer, Scopas, shows himself untrammelled by earlier Classical restraint but working wholly in the Classical mould.

From the middle group of figures on the west pediment of the Tegean Temple of Athena that Scopas carved, there survives a stupendous head of Achilles. Achilles was the archetypal warrior-hero of *The Iliad*, the prince with whose rising wrath the great epic poem opens and with whose sated wrath it ends. Although much battered, this surviving original stone head, with a lionskin helmet, still transmits Achilles' grimly murderous anger with chilling force. He is part of a group of warrior-heroes that originally included Hercules immediately to his left.

THE GOD OF LONGING

Less well known than his brother Eros, god of desire, Pothos was the god or personification of *pothos* (longing or yearning). Scopas made at least two statues of Pothos, one for Samothrace, mentioned by Pliny, and another for Megara. In depicting Pothos, Scopas adopted a gentler approach, suitable for an emotion less ravenous if perhaps less easily satisfied than Eros. This languid youth leans on one draped arm, with plump legs crossed and soulful eyes set in soft, effeminate features, all suggesting vague longing. In a broadly similar work, *Hypnos,* Scopas portrayed the god of sleep.

Above: Scopas did not solely depict women caught up in frenzy, as this beautifully calm, reflective head of Hygeia, attributed to him, shows. Hygeia was the goddess of health, daughter of the divine healer Asclepius.

Below: Hypnos, *a bronze sculpted by Fernand Khnopff in the 1890s, was based on an original head of the god of sleep by Scopas.*

LYSIPPUS
ALEXANDER'S COURT SCULPTOR

Lysippus was the most prominent, prolific and longest-lived of the great 4th-century sculptors. He was active *c*.360–*c*.305BC, reputedly making 1,500 works, all of them in bronze. Considered the most accomplished artist of his age, Lysippus suitably became Alexander the Great's favourite – in fact, court – sculptor. The world-conqueror allowed almost no one else to sculpt him. Lysippus went on to make portrait busts of many of Alexander's warring Successors, such as Cassander and Seleucus I, who founded the Seleucid Empire in 312BC. A native of Sicyon in the Peloponnese,

Above: Lysippus sculpted many bronze busts of Alexander, all since lost. This marble copy, made for the Roman Emperor Hadrian's collection at Tivoli outside Rome, captures the conqueror's ruthless determination and will mixed with his spark of romantic pothos (longing). Like most such portraits, it is probably very flattering.

Right: An ephebe (young man) from the sea off Marathon, of c.340BC. It is attributed to Lysippus or his school on stylistic grounds and dated to c.330BC. A rare bronze original, it has a graceful sweetness very different from the severity of 5th-century art.

THE *GETTY VICTOR*

An almost life-size bronze statue of a victorious young athlete, found in the Adriatic in 1964, has been associated with Lysippus or his workshop on stylistic grounds. It is very similar to the *Marathon Boy* also found in the sea off Marathon, another bronze original of *c*.330BC and now in Athens' National Museum. When sold to the Getty Museum in Malibu in 1977, the Adriatic bronze fetched $3,900,000, then a record sum for any sculpture. It has since become known as the *Getty Victor*. With their supple, relaxed, still half-boyish bodies and delicate features, both differ greatly from earlier tough super-masculine heroes.

Lysippus ran a workshop of almost industrial size that was continued after his death by his sons.

Ancient writers such as Pliny relate that Lysippus invented an entirely new canon, or mathematically calculated ideal of beauty, almost displacing that of Polyclitus. Lysippus' *Canon* postulated a smaller head, longer legs and a slender body, producing a generally more graceful, aristocratic air – exactly what his mostly royal or noble clients wanted.

Such new proportions also allowed Lysippus' statues to be viewed equally well from any angle, whereas Polyclitus' *Canon* only permitted a narrowly frontal approach. In this, as with his increasingly monarchical customers, Lysippus stands on the dividing line of the Classical and Hellenistic Ages.

THE *APOXYMENOS*

One of Lysippus' most famous and characteristic statues is the *Apoxymenos*, a young athlete scraping himself with a strigil after exercising, in the usual Greek manner. A surviving Roman copy in marble gives a good impression of this smooth-cheeked, long-limbed, young man. He is shown shifting his weight from one foot to another and stretching his right arm out, while his left hand holds the strigil. His slender body is supported by long, tensed thighs, his right leg set back with only his toes touching the ground; he hardly seems to have exerted himself at all. Such effortless elegance was novel when depicting an athlete. It was made *c.*340BC.

The statue was brought to Rome by Marcus Agrippa (63–12BC), the emperor Augustus' first minister, and set up outside the public baths he built. Later, when the emperor Tiberius removed it to his own palace, there was such an outcry from the Roman public suddenly robbed of one of its favourite artworks that even that most parsimonious of emperors had to return it.

THE *FARNESE HERCULES*

Very different but equally illustrative of Lysippus' versatile genius is the *Farnese Hercules*, which once belonged to the Farnese family in Rome. Again this is a marble copy of a bronze. It shows the semi-divine hero, a son of Zeus, wearily leaning on a tree trunk after his labours. Hercules became increasingly seen as a human role model, for he relied almost wholly on his own strength – admittedly huge – to achieve his ends, rather than divine assistance. Alexander regarded Hercules as one of his special heroes.

If weary, the hero is massively muscled, in a way inconceivable in earlier statues, the result of obsessive body-building in the gymnasium, and far from the ideal balance of earlier Classical art. In a few years his heroic muscles could easily turn to flab. Within decades such hulks would become common in Hellenistic art.

By contrast, Lysippus' *Hermes* of *c.*320BC shows the messenger god – adjusting his winged sandal on a support – as a model of easy relaxation, his stance free and elegant.

Left: The Farnese Hercules, *a marble copy of an original bronze, reveals another side of Lysippus' genius. Hercules is shown massively muscled, the result of manic body-building in the gymnasium. This is very different from the balance of earlier Classical art.*

Below: The Apoxymenos, *a young athlete scraping himself after exercise, a Roman marble copy of a bronze original. This elegant, long-limbed young man hardly seems to have exerted himself at all. It was made* c.340BC.

THE FACE OF ALEXANDER

Alexander was keenly aware of the value of his royal image, as the young, handsome and unconquered hero, divinely favoured and inspired – even possibly divinely fathered, a belief that Alexander himself may have held after his pilgrimage to the shrine of Amon-Zeus at Siwah in the Libyan desert.

Alexander commissioned many portrait busts by Lysippus. All were bronzes that have since been lost, but marble copies of several survive. Among the finest are the copy made for Hadrian's collection at his Villa at Tivoli outside Rome and one that is now in Istanbul. The former especially captures the mixture of the conqueror's ruthless determination and will with the spark of romantic *pothos* that was characteristic of Alexander. Such portraits almost certainly flattered the Macedonian king, giving him uplifted eyes, sweeping hair and a heroic air. They were widely copied after Alexander's death in 323BC.

THE HELLENISTIC GOLDEN AGE 320–200 BC

Right: The Winged Victory of Samothrace, *an original masterpiece in marble from the 3rd century* BC.

Below: The Apollo Belvedere, *a Roman copy of an original marble work of* c.320BC *attributed to Leochares. Its smooth beauty was once widely admired.*

The death of Alexander (323BC) conventionally marks the end of the Classical and the beginning of the Hellenistic ages, but there was no abrupt change in style. As the new Hellenistic kingdoms, often now of unprecedented size and wealth, established themselves as grand patrons, art began to explore new extremes, becoming more refined, more violent or more ecstatic.

THE *APOLLO BELVEDERE*

Typical of the new refinement was the *Apollo Belvedere*, carved *c.*320BC by Leochares. Leochares worked for Philip II of Macedonia and then Alexander and his Successors. He made gold and ivory statues of the older Macedonian monarch for a round temple, the Philippeion, in Olympia in a newly dramatic manner. But he was most noted for his representations of the gods, especially this *Apollo* (named after its present location). For centuries after its rediscovery in the Renaissance this marble was regarded as one of the supreme masterpieces of world art and the absolute summit of male beauty. It deeply impressed the German art critic Johann Winckelmann and the poet Goethe in the 18th century.

Tastes change. When the Elgin Marbles from the Parthenon revealed a new, less epicene and more dynamic canon of male beauty in the early 19th century, the *Apollo Belvedere* fell terminally out of fashion. But it remains, in its smooth, almost weightless way, a fine example of Hellenistic art at

its most exquisite. (It was, of course, originally painted.) Leochares also worked with Scopas, a very different artist, on the Mausoleum of Halicarnassus.

THE *WINGED VICTORY OF SAMOTHRACE*

The goddess Nike lands as if on the bow of a galley, her windswept drapery flying in the wind, her massive wings outstretched. An original marble work, she once stood on a marble carving of ship's prow in a sanctuary on the north Aegean island of Samothrace, where many Hellenistic kings commemorated successes. Probably she was set up to celebrate a great naval victory by one of Macedonia's kings, perhaps Antigonus II in the 250s BC. However, she could equally well date to about 50 years later and commemorate a Rhodian victory.

The sculptor's name remains unknown, but he was obviously inspired by Paionius' great *Nike* at Olympia of 200 years earlier.

THE *ALEXANDER SARCOPHAGUS*

The so-called *Alexander Sarcophagus* is the finest and most elaborate funerary monument to survive from the Hellenistic age. It has never, however, contained the body of Alexander the Great. This was interred in splendour in Alexandria by Ptolemy I but has long since vanished. This tomb was probably a commission made *c.*310BC for King Abdalonymus, a ruler whom Alexander had placed on the throne of Sidon in Phoenicia (Lebanon) in 333BC. The Phoenicians, although they rapidly became Hellenized, always preferred burial to cremation, then more common among the Greeks.

However, the Phoenicians employed sculptors from Greece to carve the friezes on the long sides. One shows Alexander fighting the Persians at the Battle of Issus in 333BC; the other depicts a hunt with both Macedonians and Sidonians together, so linking Abdalonymus' new regime firmly to Alexander. (Abdalonymus had been only the palace gardener originally. He ended up one of Alexander's Companions.) The reliefs have kept much of their colour, while the lid and chest are so richly adorned with finely carved metal mouldings that the sarcophagus resembles a giant jewel box.

He was also a genius, for this massive figure brims with tension and vigour. Originally 3m (9ft 9in) tall with her head, the *Nike*'s twisting axes and the contours of her wings and clothing are best viewed from below, as she was originally and now is once more in the Louvre. The statue shows Hellenistic art at its dynamic best.

THE *PHILOSOPHER'S HEAD*

Most statues were still made in bronze, however, and so have perished. One striking exception is the portrait bust found in the sea off Anticythera and probably dating from *c.*250BC. It has been called the *Philosopher's Head* because the face expresses such powerful intellectual energy and moral strength through the finely engraved beard, tousled locks and piercing gaze. Such qualities could only be fully conveyed in bronze, again emphasizing how much has been lost. The head was probably part of a group of philosophers, for other fragments have been found nearby, mostly legs and feet that seem to have been torn off a plinth. They were probably *en route* to Rome, part of some victorious general's booty.

Above: A bust found in the sea from c.250BC. *It is called the* Philosopher's Head *because the face expresses such intellectual and moral energy.*

Right: The Alexander Sarcophagus *is the finest funerary monument of the Hellenistic age, packed with vigorous battle scenes, although it never contained the actual body of Alexander. It was probably a commission made* c.310BC *for King Abdalonymus, a ruler whom Alexander had placed on the throne of Sidon in Phoenicia.*

LATER HELLENISTIC ART
200–30BC

Right: Spinario, *or* Boy Pulling a Thorn from His Foot *may date from c.200BC, or may be a later Roman copy. It reveals the age's growing taste for sentimental genre subjects. This is a composite work, for the head and the body come from different statues.*

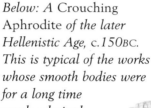

Below: A Crouching Aphrodite *of the later Hellenistic Age, c.150BC. This is typical of the works whose smooth bodies were for a long time much admired.*

After 200BC, the growing power of Rome began to affect the Greek art market. The Romans proved enthusiasts for the Baroque styles of later Hellenistic art, shipping off many artworks, frequently without paying. The influence of Greek art on Rome, for a time overwhelming, was all one way, however, for Roman art did not at this stage affect Greek artistic development. Greece's new masters simply wanted ever more copies of existing masterworks of the most blatantly dramatic or sentimental sort.

VENUS DE MILO
Typical of the age's more serene art, which today can seem bland, is the *Venus de Milo*, an original marble. The now armless statue of the goddess Aphrodite was found on the island of Melos in 1819 and taken to France, becoming world famous in the 19th century. Carved around 100BC, she has broad hips, a small head and primly arranged hair. The statue is signed by Hagesandros of Antioch, an otherwise unknown artist obviously influenced by the canonical beauty of his great predecessors Praxiteles and Lysippus. The statue was made in two parts, joined at the hips, with naturalistic drapery slipping off her finely carved naked upper body. Her missing arms may have held an Eros, often Aphrodite's companion.

A far more interesting earlier example of female beauty is *Crouching Aphrodite*, a copy of an original by Doidalsas of Bithynia. Although the goddess has lost both her

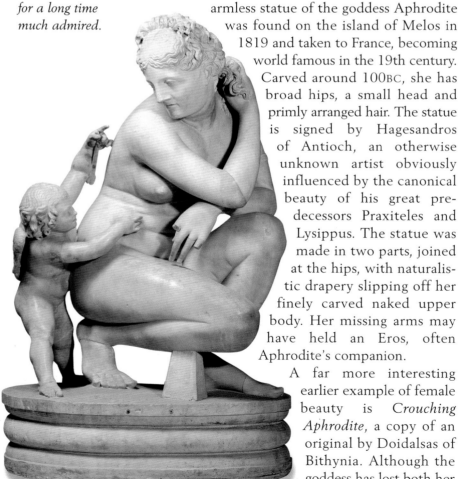

arms and the back of her head, the lovely sweep of her body as she bends, perhaps preparing to bathe, has all the naturalness of a nymph. Doidalsas' statue proved very popular and was much copied.

Among popular sculptures catering to the age's more sentimental side were small statues such as *Baby Playing with a Goose* or *Boy Pulling a Thorn from His Foot*, both of which date from *c.*200BC. Both these naked children, with their carefully brushed hair and almost Dickensian sweetness of manner, seem to be the offspring of good homes.

THE PERGAMUM ALTAR
But the age's real taste was for the melodramatic and exhibitionist. Nowhere was this better appreciated than in the newly rich kingdom of Pergamum in north-western Asia Minor. To commemorate his defeat of the invading Gauls in *c.*230BC, King Attalus I (241–197BC) erected a tremendous series of statues on

THE *LAOCOÖN'S* REDISCOVERY

In January 1506 Pope Julius I heard that some fine statues had been dug up in a vineyard near the ruins of Nero's palace in Rome. He ordered Sangallo, one of his architects, to inspect the statue. Sangallo invited Michelangelo, recently returned to Rome, along. Before they had even got off their horses, they agreed that the group must be the *Laocoön* praised by Pliny the Elder. Michelangelo later said that the discovery inspired him to portray spiritual anguish and physical torment through violent muscular movement. Many later artists, including El Greco, were influenced by the *Laocoön*. The statue is a copy of an original of *c.*180BC made probably in *c.*50BC by three sculptors: Agesander, Polydorus and Athenodorus of Rhodes, who created sensational works for the Roman market. The myth illustrated was retold in *The Aeneid* by Virgil. The priest Laocoön had warned the Trojans about the Greeks' wooden horse. His attempt to deflect the fated course of events angered the gods, who sent sea serpents to destroy him and his sons. The carving's amazing naturalism is typically late Hellenistic. (A recent theory that this is a fake made by Michelangelo himself has been generally discounted.)

Below: This Laocoön *group is a copy of an original of c.180BC made c.50BC by three sculptors of Rhodes, who created sensational works for the Roman market. The myth illustrated was later retold in* The Aeneid *by Virgil.*

Pergamum's citadel. Epigonus created the bronze *Dying Gaul*, a Gallic man propping himself up on his right arm to look at his fatal wound. Although we again have only a marble copy, it remains a brilliant study in anatomy and psychology, the wound most realistically sculpted. Epigonus also made the *Chieftain Killing Himself and His Wife*, an even more dramatic double piece showing a Gallic noble committing suicide rather than surrender.

The crowning achievement of the Attalid dynasty, and of Hellenistic baroque, was the vast Altar of Zeus, erected between 180 and 160BC, now in Berlin. Menecrates was among the named

artists but many more were probably involved. The huge frieze, 121m (400ft) long, that encircles the base of the altar depicts a *gigantomachia*, a battle of the giants and gods. By casting this as the victory of Hellenism over barbarous Gauls, the Pergameme kings could justify their unpopular rule over the cities of Ionia.

The place of honour in the centre of the east frieze shows Zeus hurling a thunderbolt at Porphyrion, a serpent-footed giant. Elsewhere, Athena seizes a young winged giant by the hair, while below, sunk in the ground, Ge, mother of the giants, begs for mercy. The whole frieze surges with dynamic energy.

Below: The Altar of Zeus at Pergamum was the most spectacular work of the Hellenistic baroque, built between 180 and 160BC.

CHAPTER V

VASE PAINTING

While Greek pottery ranks among the finest in the world, vase painting was for the Greeks themselves a secondary form of art compared to painted panels and murals. These depicted events of grand historical or mythical importance. However, almost no Greek paintings before the 4th century BC have survived. By contrast, numerous vases survive from the Bronze Age on, giving fresh perspectives on the daily lives and beliefs of the Greeks.

Pottery has survived so well partly because its shards are nearly indestructible. Vases have been found in quantity over a wide area, for the Greeks seldom used glassware or other types of containers. Instead, they stored their wine, olive oil and water in vases and pots, and also exported their products, principally olive oil, around the Mediterranean in pottery of increasing splendour and magnificence. Often the container must have been more valuable than its contents, although Greek olive oil and wines were appreciated by the Etruscans, Gauls (in both France and northern Italy) and by the Romans.

At first, Corinth was the greatest exporter of vases, but during the mid-6th century BC, Athens replaced it as the chief producer of the best pottery. Athens continued to dominate the market for high-quality painted vases until the mid-4th century BC. By then, the golden age of vase-making was coming to an end, although opulent ware continued to be produced for long after.

Left: An Athenian red figure vase (on a black base) by the 'Niobid Painter' c.460BC, showing battling giants and gods.

BRONZE AGE VASES
1800–1100BC

Above: A Kamares-style cup. Pottery of almost china-like delicacy was produced in Crete at the time of the early palaces c.2000–1700BC.

The lively civilization of Minoan Crete produced colourful and vivid pottery throughout the 2nd millennium BC, the period of its great palaces. Minoan pottery styles – meticulously ranked by Arthur Evans (the archaeologist who rediscovered Cnossus Palace in 1900) into categories that not everyone, however, now accepts – show a culture reaching its peak around 1500BC. Soon after, Mycenaean Greeks from the mainland became dominant in Crete and across the whole Aegean. In their pottery, as in their other arts, the Mycenaeans essentially continued Minoan styles but in stiffer, more stylized and anthropocentric ways. But it can be hard to distinguish between the two civilizations' artefacts.

THE FIRST MINOAN STYLES
Pottery was the first art form in which the Minoan genius revealed its tremendous imaginative powers. The early style, called Kamares, probably originated in Phaestus, the main palace in southern Crete, but was discovered by archaeologists in the Kamares Cave, a burial site.

Kamares-style pottery is characterized by varied abstract spiral and curvilinear designs and dark mottled colours, combining drawings on the surface of the vase with varied relief patterns. These are mostly floral or zoomorphic (depicting animals). The human form is notably absent from this early art.

This style flourished at the time of the early palaces c.2000–1700BC, producing at its finest the so-called 'eggshell' ware. Thrown on the potter's wheel, such cups were designed to imitate the fine metal ware that has not generally survived. But they achieve a delicacy almost anticipating that of genuine china, which to many suggests a feminine influence typical of Minoan culture in general. What much Minoan art apparently lacks is the insistence on symmetry that would characterize later Greek art. Some time around 1700BC a major cataclysm, probably an earthquake, totally destroyed all the Cretan palaces. They were soon rebuilt on a grander, more systematic scale, and at the same time Cretan pottery entered its finest stage.

THE MINOAN ZENITH
Typical of Minoan vase painting at its liveliest and most naturalistic is the *Dendra Vase*, across whose curves an alarmingly lifelike octopus spreads

Left: An octopus design on the Dendra Vase, *produced c.1500BC at the apex of Minoan civilization. It reflects both the Cretans' love of the sea and their brilliantly fluid art.*

its tentacles. Similar vases are decorated with plants. They reflect both Cretan fascination with sea life – the Minoans were great sailors and fishermen – and their love of free-flowing forms. But the human image now figured also.

Three famous low reliefs, all of which would probably have been painted originally, come from Aghia Triada, a royal villa near Phaestus. They are the *Chieftain Cup*, the *Boxer Vase* and the *Harvester Vase*. All are decorated with typical serpentine patterns, giving vivid glimpses into life in Bronze Age Crete. The *Harvester Vase* in particular portrays cheerful peasants without the condescension that might be expected in an art normally geared to courtiers' tastes. A common decorative motif from Cnossus of this period is the lily, found on many vases, but the most frequent motifs feature spirals, animals, birds and fishes, depicted almost impressionistically.

All these are dated to the 'Late Minoan I' period of *c.*1550–1450BC, the seeming zenith of Minoan culture. It seems probable – although no consensus has been established – that the volcanic eruption of Thira cut short Minoan culture just as it was flowering.

THE ART OF THE MYCENAEANS

Despite their cultural debts to the Minoans, the Greek Mycenaeans favoured a markedly more militaristic art than the Cretans. This is immediately obvious in the *Chariot Krater* (mixing bowl) from Cnossus of *c.*1400BC. In the chariot, the 'tank of the Bronze Age', two tall, long-robed figures stand behind the pair of horses. The portrayal of the two horses follows Mycenaean customs in vase painting: the artist, trying to show the chariot seen head on in perspective, has painted only one horse's body, but this has two tails, two pairs of hind legs and forelegs and two heads. The whole scene has a stiffness about it

quite distinct from Minoan naturalness. So do the grandiose 'Palace-style' vases of the Mycenaean period at Cnossus.

From Mycenae itself in the 13th century BC comes the *Vase with Warriors*. This shows six helmeted soldiers with shields and helmets marching off, a woman in the background seeming to lament their parting. However, any intended pathos is undermined by the almost comically inept art.

Dating from *c.*1200BC, a terracotta vase shows an octopus, a creature loved by Minoan artists but that has here become heavily stylized. Similarly, a charging bull on a terracotta krater from Enkomi in Cyprus of *c.*1180BC retains nothing of the magnificent vitality of earlier bulls but is simply a schematic, nearly monochrome reminder of flesh-and-blood bulls. Some archaeologists think that only when Mycenaean vase painting is almost identical to Minoan does it really succeed as an art form. Others see in such simplified works the precursors of Geometric art.

Above: A Palace-style vase, made c.1400BC when Crete was under Mycenaean rule, is altogether stiffer in approach.

Below: This terracotta krater, showing a bull charging a bird, comes from Enkomi in Cyprus. It dates to the Late Mycenaean period c.1180BC.

PROTOGEOMETRIC AND GEOMETRIC ART c.1050–700BC

Right: The revival of Greek economic, social and artistic life in the 8th century BC led to the return of figurative art, albeit in a very stylized form, as the sketchy, diagrammatic figures on this terracotta vase from the Middle Geometric period reveal.

After 1200BC the elaborate palace-centred culture of Mycenae, with its bureaucracies, elegantly dressed courtiers, extensive trade routes and trading contacts with Egypt and the Levant, began to collapse. Traditionally this was due to Dorian invasions from the north, but other reasons, including civil wars and even climate change, have been suggested. By 1100BC Mycenaean civilization had vanished almost completely. In its place came a simpler, more parochial way of life. Art soon reflected this change, abandoning the increasingly feeble Mycenaean attempts at realism in favour of an austere style that at times approached abstraction.

Most pottery in the early centuries after 1100BC comes from Athens, the one major Mycenaean city that, according to legend, escaped total destruction. Within the shelter afforded by the walls of the Acropolis, Geometric art seems to have been born. The Diplyon Cemetery (named after the gate in the walls of classical Athens) has revealed many artefacts from this era.

Below: The stiff, twig-like figures in this detail from the great vase opposite may depict chariot races held in honour of the dead, mentioned in Homer's The Iliad.

PROTOGEOMETRIC: THE ART OF SURVIVORS

The first new style to emerge is called Protogeometric. Artists continued to use Mycenaean shapes, but with decorations restricted to circles, semicircles, rhombuses, crosses and hooks, arranged in bands. These designs were drawn using brushes fixed to compasses, marking a completely fresh approach to art. The ground (base colour) of the vases was generally light-coloured with decorations added in black gloss or glaze. Some Protogeometric vases may come from Cyprus, to which many Mycenaeans had fled. Such a limited range of decoration, devoid of human or animal figures, suited an age struggling for survival.

EARLY GEOMETRIC: THE FIRST AWAKENING

As Greek economic and cultural life began very tentatively to revive after 900BC, potters took to experimenting again. While they abandoned compass-controlled arcs in favour of grouped zigzags and obliques, they initially kept the mainly black base of the Protogeometric period. Decoration was increasingly organized into metopes (or panels), within which geometric patterns, especially the typically Greek shape of the *meander* (or Greek key design), were painted. Finally, artists began creating simple, silhouetted figures of animals.

An early example comes from a Cretan burial urn, which depicts some alarmingly feral creatures – possibly wild cats, but more probably creatures from some nightmarish myth. However, Athens remained the chief source of pottery. Horses, then very important in a Greek world that was strongly aristocratic, are among the first recognizable animals to appear on vases.

THE MIDDLE GEOMETRIC: THE HUMAN FORM RETURNS

By 800BC the tempo of Greek life was beginning to quicken. The century was to witness the real rebirth of Greece, with the writing of Homer's poetry, the invention of the Greek alphabet (derived from Phoenician examples), the beginnings of colonization and the establishment of great festivals such as the Olympic Games in 776BC.

This resurgence encouraged the reappearance of human forms, albeit still in rigidly geometrized form. Strange, stick-like figures gradually began to fill more and more of the vase areas. They also became freer and less rigid, although they long remained highly stylized.

Large burial urns containing the ashes of important people (cremation was then the normal form of burial, in contrast to the Mycenaean preference for inhumation) often carried scenes of mourning. One of these, a terracotta krater about 1.5m (5ft)

high dating from *c.*750BC, shows a funeral procession in the top band with a corpse lying on a bier, with identical stylized human forms on the other side. But the lower band rejoices in a multitude of figures, who seem to be wearing odd kilts or skirts. They are driving carts or more probably chariots. It is possible that they are meant to be competitors taking part in the deceased's funeral games. This typically Greek custom was by then widely established, at least according to Homer's poetry.

This grand vase is often attributed to the 'Hirschfeld Painter'. (Potters are often named after particular works, another example being the 'Diplyon Artist'). However, we know nothing at all definite about this putative potter. Even this particular vase may not have been the work of one individual.

THE LATE GEOMETRIC

By the Late Geometric period (750–700BC), decoration had spread to cover the entire surface of vases, with busy friezes of animals and humans. However, Geometric art, which had allowed the revival of decorative vase painting in a characteristically Greek form, strongly emphasizing symmetry, had by the century's end reached an artistic dead-end.

What had been necessary astringency after the collapse of Mycenaean art was in danger of becoming a straitjacket. Greek art needed a fresh direction and an injection of vitality. Both would come from Asia, then far more advanced.

Below: Standing 1.2m (4ft) high, this terracotta Late Geometric krater by the Hirschfield painter from Attica is the finest burial urn from the 8th century BC. Such urns marked the burial pits in which cremated bodies were placed. The vase actually shows a grand funeral cortège with a long row of warriors in their chariots.

IDEAS FROM THE EAST
c.720–570BC

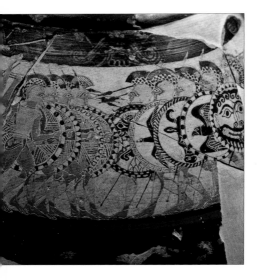

Above: The Chigi Vase, *a very fine Corinthian-style vase with a triple tier of friezes, dates from c.620BC. It is made of terracotta with a dark and light glaze of paint, and covered in red and white figures of hoplite soldiers.*

Below: Corinth emerged as the greatest centre of vase-making c.700BC. On this skyphos (drinking cup) of c.670BC from Kameiros in Rhodes, a black dog lollops with lithe energy across a white surface – an example of Corinthian art at its vivid best.

The 7th century BC saw major changes in pottery painting. Although in some cities potters for a time retained Geometric motifs, elsewhere they began experimenting with new ways of depicting figures. They also discovered new, much more interesting subjects. (Possibly earlier artists were also illustrating myths and legends, but their starkly silhouetted forms make any narrative almost impossibly hard to discern.)

Greek artists began to borrow the flora and fauna motifs of Syria. The protypes of these may have first been introduced by the Phoenicians, then masters of the Mediterranean, and adapted by them for their own purposes.

Syrian polychromatic influence merged with the perennial Greek insistence on form to create the colourful 'orientalizing' art of the 7th century BC. The flourishing Isthmian port of Corinth, which was founding colonies across the Mediterranean, became for the next 100 years the leading centre of artistic innovation. Pottery styles are named after its innovatory use of clear-cut forms, although Athens always remained an important centre for ceramics.

Above: The Polyphemus Amphora *of c.680BC, fussily proto-Attic in style, illustrates the story of Odysseus blinding the drunken giant Polyphemus on its top frieze, while lower down animals run wild. Underneath them the Gorgons pursue Perseus, who has just killed their sister Medusa, in quite another myth.*

PROTOCORINTHIAN 720–640BC

A new interest in depicting myths and legends – which merged into religion and history – led to scenes filled with griffins, sphinxes and sirens. Homer's epics, *The Iliad* and *Odyssey*, quickly known all round the Greek world,

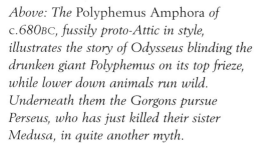

became one of the prime sources of myths for potters. The *Polyphemus Amphora* of *c*.680BC, found in a child's grave at Eleusis near Athens, illustrates the story of Odysseus blinding the drunken giant Polyphemus on its top frieze, while lower down animals run wild. Underneath them the Gorgons, the lethal sisters of decapitated Medusa, pursue Perseus, who has just killed the snake-headed horror, in quite another myth. Stylistically the vase is called proto-Attic. Despite its richness of detail, it lacks the purity of line of the best Corinthian work.

Much simpler in theme and artistically far more powerful is the *skyphos* (drinking cup) of *c*.670BC from Kameiros in Rhodes. The long black form of a dog lollops with superb energy across a white surface. This is a true Corinthian work, as is the *aryballos* (perfume flask) of *c*.650BC from Thebes. Its head is formed like a lion's mouth with savage fangs, while on its body hoplites are vividly depicted fighting with spears and shields. Such potent works typify the Protocorinthian style in its maturity.

THE *CHIGI VASE*

Perhaps the finest example of the Corinthian style is the *Chigi Vase*, with its triple tier of friezes. Dating from *c*.620BC, the vase, of a type called an *oinochoe* (wine-pourer), is made of terracotta with dark and light glaze paint covered in red and white figures. It comes from Formello near Veii, an important Etruscan city. The topmost frieze graphically depicts two armies approaching each other in battle formation. This vase also provides invaluable information about early hoplite warfare.

Below this scene a second frieze shows a procession of horsemen, chariots, a lion hunt and the Judgement of Paris. (The Trojan prince had had to make a perilous choice of deities: who was the most beautiful, Aphrodite, Athena or Hera? Choosing Aphrodite, the love goddess, he incurred the undying hatred of the other two, a fatal choice that ultimately led to the fall of Troy. A sphinx meanwhile looks on impartially.) The bottom frieze shows a hare hunt. Figures are now no longer just bare silhouettes but are portrayed with a true muscular vigour.

THE 'NESSOS PAINTER'

A vase-painter known to us as the 'Nessos Painter' from his masterpiece, a huge amphora some 1.2m (4ft) tall depicting the legend of Hercules and Nessos, flourished in Attica in the late 7th century BC. Painted only on one side, this bears the names of Heracles (Hercules) and Netos (Nessos) above it for the first time. It illustrates a popular myth. Hercules, the archetypal hero, was escorting Deianeria, a princess, when Nessos, a centaur who worked as a ferryman, tried to rape her. Hercules is shown on the amphora's neck seizing the centaur by his neck and killing him. Deianeria later gave Hercules a shirt soaked in Nessos' poisoned blood, thinking it was a love potion. Maddened by the torment of the 'shirt of Nessos', the hero killed himself on a funeral pyre.

The story is painted with far more artistic verve and self-confidence than on earlier vases. So too is the lower story, again of the Gorgons chasing Perseus. Instead of the robotic figures shown on the *Polyphemus Amphora* of 70 years earlier, these monsters are depicted as horrific winged demons in hot pursuit of Perseus, who is not even present.

With masters like the 'Nessos Painter' working in Attica, Athens again displaced Corinth as the main manufacturer of vases, a position it retained until the end of the Classical Age. The potters' quarter in Athens was known as the Kerameikos, after its clay (ceramic) vase-makers.

Below: A vase-painter known as the 'Nessos Painter' produced this masterpiece, a huge amphora, 1.2m (4ft) tall, depicting the legend of Hercules and Nessos, in the late 7th century BC. Painted only on one side, this bears the names of Heracles (Hercules) and Netos (Nessos) above it for the first time.

CLASSICISM AND NATURALISM 570–480BC

As Athens emerged as the chief pottery centre *c*.570BC – just when Solon's economic and social reforms were starting to have beneficial effects – its individual artists developed the black figure style (on a red or pale ground) to its effective limits. Some artists then went on to pioneer red figure vases on a black ground. Although this was technically harder, it permitted the depiction of increasingly naturalistic and powerful scenes. With this style, Greek vase painting was to reach its zenith. Artists now often signed their vases, thus demonstrating a novel self-confidence.

Among the earlier notable works is the *François Vase* of *c*.560BC, a grand krater exported to Etruria. Signed by the potter Ergotimos and the painter Cleitias, its six friezes brim with mythological scenes, many relating the story of Achilles, the warrior-hero of *The Iliad*.

Cleitias signed many other works, as did Sophilos, who was both a painter and potter. This was now an increasingly common and effective combination.

Above: Among the grandest Attic vases of the 6th century is the François Vase *(named after its finder), a krater exported to Etruria. Signed by the potter Ergotimos and the painter Cleitias, its friezes brim with mythological scenes, many about Achilles, the warrior-hero.*

EXEKIAS THE MASTER

One of the age's greatest potter-cum-painters, some 30 pieces are attributed to Exekias. He worked between 550 and 520BC. Among his masterpieces are *Dionysus in a Ship*, a terracotta glazed *kylix* (cup) of *c*.540BC. The bearded wine god – only later was Dionysus shown as a beardless youth – lolls at ease in his ship, a drinking horn in his hands. The ship's mast is sprouting vines that bear luscious fruit above, while around cavort dolphins. The scene brims with joyful lyricism.

Different, but equally masterly, is *Ajax and Achilles*, showing the two heroes intent on a board game during a break in the Trojan Wars (not a scene mentioned by Homer). It demonstrates Exekias' skill in incised lines, which allowed greater realism in depicting armour and flesh. Also notable are his innovatory composition, with the strong diagonals formed by the spears, and the intimate subject-matter. Exekias was the first to paint such scenes from legend as complete pictures, and his work is often considered to make him the first great individual in Western art. But such black figure vases were inherently limited, for they lacked chromatic variety. To create this meant reversing the age-old formula of painting in the figures while leaving the background untouched.

Left: Ajax and Achilles, *showing the two heroes intent on a game during a break in the Trojan Wars, demonstrates Exekias' skill in incised lines, which allowed greater realism in depicting armour and flesh. Also notable are his innovatory composition, with the strong diagonals formed by the spears, and intimate subject-matter. As the first to paint such scenes as complete pictures, Exekias is sometimes considered the first great individual Western painter.*

THE RED FIGURE PIONEERS

In about 530BC Athenian painters pioneered the development of red figure vases, a truly revolutionary move. (Black figure works continued to be produced for a while as well, however.) The first such vase is attributed to Andocides, possibly a pupil of Exekias, who signed an amphora on which one side has red figures and the other has black figures, both showing Hercules reclining on a couch.

Among the best of the new painters-cum-potters, a group today called the Pioneers, was Euphronius. About 510BC he painted a kylix depicting Leagros, a beautiful youth riding a skittish horse with calm self-confidence. This shows a great advance in naturalism, as does his more elaborate vase showing the death of Sarpedon, a Trojan prince. Euphronius also depicted figures reclining at a *symposium* (party) with innovatory accuracy on a *psykter* (wine cooler). The diners' half-naked bodies, even the pupils of their eyes, are remarkably lifelike.

There was keen competition among these painters, who must have known each other in the still small polis. Euthymides, a contemporary, inscribed a vase with his name and the boast: "As Euphronius could never have made it."

SOSIAS

One of the finest pieces of the period is a kylix by Sosias, a painter-cum-potter working in Athens around 500BC. It shows Achilles bandaging his comrade Patroclus' wounded arm (a scene inspired by, but not actually in, Homer's *The Iliad*). Sosios has painted Patroclus in such a way – his right leg bent, his left leg stretched out before him – that he fills the curve of the vase perfectly. Patroclus looks away in well-expressed pain as Achilles concentrates on his task. The faces and bodies of each warrior are shown in naturalistic perspective, marking a final break with Archaic art's frontalism.

The Dionysiac scenes painted on an amphora in c.490BC by the 'Cleophrades Painter' (also called Epictetus), a pupil of

Euthymides, portrays the orgiastic rites of the wine god with great vigour. Dionysus, bearded and with his usual attributes of ivy and vine, is wearing long robes under which his legs move visibly, the first time that drapery was shown flowing realistically around a body. Around him, long-robed Maenads, the god's ecstatic followers, fend off impish satyrs.

The extensive use of a diluted glaze is also striking. Above, on the jar's neck, naked athletes compete. Attic potters' achievement of classical naturalism now matched that of contemporary sculptors and, presumably, panel painters.

Above: Dionysus in a Ship, *a terracotta glazed kylix of* c.540BC, *one of Exekias's 30 known masterpieces. The wine god lolls at ease in his ship, a drinking horn in his hands, while the mast sprouts vines bearing fruit and dolphins cavort around.*

Right: Achilles and Patroclus *by Sosias, a painter-cum-potter working in Athens around 500BC. Among the finest early red figure vases, it shows Achilles bandaging his comrade Patroclus' wounded arm (a scene not actually in* The Iliad*).*

ZENITH AND DECLINE
480–340BC

The Athenians emerged from the Persian wars (490–478BC) triumphant if battered. Rebuilding their wrecked city, they founded a new League against Persia, which soon became their empire, and completed their own progress to full democracy. This political upsurge was matched by artistic advances.

In painting, this was best exemplified by the large panel paintings of Polygnotus of Thasos. While all these have vanished, some fine vase paintings that survive are thought to be very similar in general design and approach.

Among these is a vase by an artist called the 'Niobe Painter' after another vase by him depicting the death of Niobe's children. His masterpiece of about 460BC shows Athena, goddess of the city, flanked by heroes, including Theseus, Athens' legendary king, and the muscular champion Hercules with his club. The vase probably commemorates

Above: The Pan Painter in c.450BC depicted a scene of heroic legend: Hercules killing the Egyptian king Busiris, who had intended to sacrifice him. The neat hairstyle and taut strength of the Greek hero contrast with the flabby ugliness of his opponents, perhaps reflecting Athens' aggressive new self-confidence at the time.

BURIAL VASES
One form of vase differed from the general run of black figure vases: the *lekythos*, literally an oil-flask with a white ground used for weddings or, more often, funerals. These cylindrical vases were made mostly from the 450s to the 420s BC. Among them is some of the finest Attic painted pottery. The 'Achilles Painter' is known also for his superb white-ground *lekythoi*. One shows a Muse on Mount Helicon (the rock is conveniently labelled) playing her lyre. The clear, simple lines of the young woman are timelessly classical. Other lekythoi could be more colourful but all remained relatively simple.

the Battle of Marathon, Athens' first victory over the Persians in 490BC. In that battle, Theseus and other long-dead heroes were rumoured to have returned to fight alongside living Athenians. The figures are not painted in perspective or as part of a whole narrative but are isolated around the vase, as was probably then the style in mural painting too.

HEROES AND AMAZONS
More dramatically interesting is the *Amazonomachia* (Battle of the Amazons) on a resplendent krater 75cm (2ft 6in) high. This popular legend – of the defeat of the attack on Athens by the Amazons, those warrior-women who so inverted Greek ideas about women's proper role – gave artists the licence to depict

Left: A detail from the large red figure vase opposite above, showing the goddess Demeter, the goddess of wheat and agriculture, in her chariot with Triptolemus, a prince. Red figure painting allowed much clearer lines against the black ground.

THE 'ACHILLES PAINTER'

During the period of Pericles' dominance of Athenian politics, in the high noon of Athenian democracy – around 450–430BC when the Parthenon with its superb sculptures was being built – an artist known as the 'Achilles Painter' also brought vase painting to its peak. He is so-called because of an amphora attributed to him showing *Achilles and Briseis*, the Homeric hero and the slave girl, another scene inspired by *The Iliad*. His compositions are simple, usually with just a couple of isolated but serene figures who radiate the same graceful nobility as Pheidias' great sculptures of the same period. Because of this, the 'Achilles Painter' is often considered the most deeply classical vase-painter of the High Classical period. About 200 surviving vases have, with varying degrees of certainty, been ascribed to him. Many lesser painters were reputedly his pupils. With him, Attic vase painting reached its peak.

DECLINE AND DECADENCE

Although fine vases continued to be made in the late 5th century BC in Athens, the 4th century BC saw a general decline in standards. In Athens artistic interest now increasingly focused on making vases in metals, including silver and even gold. But in Greek cities in southern Italy, lavish pottery vases such as the *Alcestis Vase* continued to be made.

Increasingly, these vases were floridly decorated with often flabby designs. Only when illustrating low-life scenes from theatrical comedy – as on a vase from Paestum, which shows actors with grotesque masks – can these painters be considered really successful.

half-naked women. It also served as a parable for the recent defeat of Persia, another non-Hellenic invader. The scene is crowded with violent action as armoured Athenians spear and hack at the Amazons, who are dressed as lightly as Scythian archers.

Above, on the vase's neck, in contrast, diners are shown peacefully drinking and listening to flute girls. *The Pan Painter* around 450BC depicted another scene of heroic massacre, Hercules killing the Ethiopian king Busiris, who had intended to sacrifice *him*.

A rather different scene of legendary violence on a *skyphos* or drinking cup shows Odysseus, home from his long wanderings, shooting his mighty bow at the suitors who had long been plaguing his wife Penelope. The Homeric hero is depicted on one side of the skyphos while the terrified suitors, one with an arrow sticking into him, cower from the returning king on the other. Dating from *c*.450BC, this piece achieves its impact with notably simple, uncluttered forms.

Below: A lekythos, an oil-flask with figures on a white ground, was used for weddings and especially funerals. The clear, simple lines of the woman playing her lyre are very classical. Other lekythoi could be more colourful but all remained relatively simple.

CHAPTER VI

WALL PAINTINGS AND MOSAICS

The Greeks admired their painters as much as their sculptors. This may not now be apparent from artworks in museums, where statues predominate, but no real Greek painting before the mid-4th century BC survives. Instead, we must rely on descriptions by later writers such as Pliny, and what can be guessed from contemporary vases. We would have even less idea of Greek painting were it not for the eruption of Vesuvius in AD79, that preserved Pompeii and Herculaneum so well.

Pompeii is hugely important because, although never a Greek colony, it was very open to Greek cultural influences. Many of its houses were decorated with copies of Hellenistic masterpieces, often made by actual Greek artists. These works provide vivid examples of Greek painting in its illusionistic prime. Helped by recent discoveries from royal tombs in Macedonia and examples from houses in Rome, we can now see what master painters the Greeks were, even though they never fully grasped the principle of single unitary perspective that has underpinned realist Western art since the Renaissance. However painting in the Greek world starts far earlier with Minoan murals, some preserved by the volcanic eruption at Thira.

Left: Among the greatest of ancient paintings, The Finding of Telephus *at Herculaneum copies a work from Pergamum.*

MINOAN AND MYCENAEAN PAINTING 1700–1200BC

Above: Typical of Minoan art, this c.1550BC mural of a woman with big eyes and hair is now called La Parisienne. *She was probably a courtier, possibly a priestess.*

Below: The Prince with the Lilies *of c.1500BC, a superb relief fresco, shows a young noble in an elaborate gold headdress of great courtliness.*

The art of the Bronze-Age Aegean Minoans and Mycenaeans forms a prelude to Greek art proper. While it is uncertain how much, if any, influence their paintings had on later Greek art, one convention certainly survived: that of depicting women as white-skinned and most men as tanned brown.

Minoan paintings have been found in Crete and southern Aegean islands. In the Second Palace period (*c.*1700–1400BC), the Minoans produced wonderfully vivid and free-flowing, if hardly naturalistic, art. (Their colouring was not realistic and they gracefully elongated the human form, while the whole eye is often visible on faces painted in profile, an anatomical impossibility.) Minoan art also showed a keen awareness of non-human nature.

In all this it differed radically from the monumental art of contemporary Egypt and the Near East, areas that the Minoans knew. Cretan artists, uninterested in attempting to overawe spectators, delighted in celebrating life's fleeting pleasures. They generally painted frescoes, that is they applied pigment directly onto wet plaster, as did many Greek and Renaissance artists later. This technique, feasible only in dry climates, is well suited to painting quickly.

PALACE FRESCOES

Among earlier frescoes is a mural called *The Saffron Gatherer* from the palace at Cnossus of *c.*1600BC. Restored originally by Arthur Evans to represent a human being, it is now thought to depict a monkey picking saffron in a field. Larger and livelier at 80cm (2ft 8in) high is the *Bull-leaping Fresco* from the east wing of the great palace of *c.*1500BC. With its border painted to imitate marble, this grand mural illustrates a rite at the heart of Cretan life, the bull game, played by girls as well as boys, both sexes wearing kilts.

THE PRINCE WITH THE LILIES

A courtly, even decadent, note is struck by the superb relief fresco *The Prince with the Lilies*, showing a young noble with a huge golden headdress in almost hieratic pose. More typically Minoan in its vivacity is the *Running Officer*, showing a man leading a row of African guards, all sprinting. Typical also is the woman with big eyes and elaborate hair called *La Parisienne* (*The Parisian Woman*) who was perhaps a priestess.

In the room Evans called the Queen's Bathroom, dolphins leap gracefully around the royal bathtub – the sea was always important to the Minoans. There are few signs of war or warriors until the palace's very last phase, when it was under Mycenaean rule. From that period date the griffins, noble if stylized beasts flanking the throne of Minos.

THE THIRA MURALS

The volcanic eruption at Thira around 1500BC (some geologists prefer an earlier date) has kept the murals in houses on that once wealthy island dazzlingly fresh. These provide different views of the Bronze-Age world from the Cretan palace murals, although painted in the same style: two boys (judging by their brown colouring) are boxing; blue monkeys (unmistakeable simians, this time) clamber up rocks, fleeing pursuing dogs; butterflies and swallows flit among tree-tops; a woman, elegant in Minoan dress with small waist and puffed sleeves, is gathering saffron; antelopes brush against each other's flanks – all are scenes pulsing with vitality. The inhabitants of Thira were presumably merchants, not kings, but many murals rivals those of Crete itself. There is nothing provincial here.

Nor were they always as peace-loving as the Cretans have been assumed to be. Other frescoes show the fleet – of Thira, or

perhaps of all the Aegean islands – sailing off to visit and sometimes attack other cities. Some of these are thought to be in north Africa, revealing again the Minoans' links with Africa. The grand cycle of murals depicting the fleet's actions reveals a whole vanished Mediterranean world.

MYCENAEAN ART

The Mycenaeans, the Minoans' artistic as well as political heirs, continued the mural tradition. Unfortunately, many of their finest frescoes, such as those adorning the Palace of Nestor at Pylos in the south-western Peloponnese, were lost when that noblest of Achaean palaces was sacked. However, at Mycenae and Tiryns enough remains to give some idea of their art. As might be expected, it was often concerned with war and hunting.

From the Mycenean fort of Tiryns comes a fine example of a boar hunt, showing long-bodied hounds leaping on their prey, a scene painted with almost Minoan vivacity. The dogs' elegant collars suggest a lighter side to Mycenaean life than is often apparent. Stiffer and more stylized, but still impressive, are frescoes from Mycenae itself portraying ladies of the court, all dressed in Minoan fashion. These murals are thought to date from the late 13th century BC, shortly before the sudden collapse of Mycenaean civilization.

Above: A fresco from Thira, the volcano-blasted island, showing the Aegean fleet at sea, perhaps approaching the coast of north Africa.

Below left: This colourful, lively fresco from a mural in a house on Thira was probably painted about 1600BC. It shows monkeys clambering up rocks.

Below right: A boar hunt from a mural in the Mycenaean fortress of Tiryns, painted in the 13th century BC.

CLASSICAL PAINTING
480–320 BC

Above: The Abduction of Persephone, *a mural from a tomb at Vergina (Edessa, the oldest Macedonian capital), dates from c.330 BC. Only recently excavated, it is one of the very few Greek murals extant. Its light brush strokes convey the terror of Persephone as bearded Hades carries her off in his chariot to the underworld. Nicomachus, an artist praised by Pliny, probably painted this.*

Athens' pivotal role in the Greeks' grand victories over Persia from 490 to 479 BC called for public commemoration. Polygnotus of Thasos, who worked *c.*470–440 BC in Athens, was widely considered the first great Greek painter.

Polygnotus painted large pictures, mostly about semi-historical legends or religious myths, filled with numerous figures but little in the way of background landscape. Tentative reconstructions of his great *Sack of Troy*, which he painted for the Cnidians' Temple at Delphi, show a triple frieze of seemingly unconnected figures. As Polygnotus painted wholly on perishable wood panels, none of his work has survived.

MASTERS OF REALISM

Zeuxis of Heraclea in southern Italy, who worked *c.*435–390 BC, was considered the supreme painter of his age and a master of verisimilitude. According to one story, when asked to paint a picture of Helen of Troy, whose dazzling beauty had caused the Trojan War, he assembled the city's five most beautiful women and combined their finest features into one ideal figure. This story, whether or not literally true, suggests that, like contemporary sculptors, Zeuxis aimed at depicting an idealized human form realistically, not at portraying actual individuals. Zeuxis, too, painted only on wooden panels, which have not survived.

Zeuxis' rival was Parrhasius of Ephesus, a master of realism so convincing that his work approached *trompe l'oeil*. According to Pliny, Zeuxis painted a picture of some grapes that were so lifelike that birds came to peck at them. But Parrhasius, when called to draw back the curtain concealing his rival's work, revealed that the curtain itself was a stunningly realistic painting. Again, nothing remains of his art, but he was reputedly also skilled at depicting facial expressions.

THE 4TH-CENTURY MASTERS

After 400 BC, the heroic tendency to idealize in art began to slacken, although it always remained powerful. Nicias of Athens was a friend and pupil of the famous sculptor Praxiteles, some of whose statues he coloured. Renowned for his skill in *chiaroscuro* (dramatically juxtaposed shade and light), he painted many female figures in dramatic situations. Nothing by him survives either.

As power shifted north to Macedonia in the mid-4th century BC, Philip II and then Alexander the Great became the main artistic patrons in the Greek world.

Born *c.*380 BC in Colophon in Ionia, Apelles was considered the age's greatest artist. He was court painter to both the kings, who realized the propaganda value of his work. Alexander reputedly so

Left: Lion Hunt, *dated* c.320–300 BC, *is from Pella, the Macedonian capital. Signed by Gnosis, a renowned artist, it shows two naked youths, one Alexander the Great and the other perhaps his friend Craterus, attacking a lion. Such dramatic realism must have been common also in the wall paintings now lost.*

admired his painter that when Apelles fell in love with Pancapse, then the current royal mistress whose portrait he was painting, Alexander gave her to the artist. Or so the story goes. Apelles worked mostly in the eastern Aegean when he was not following Alexander's conquering path across Asia.

About 30 works by Apelles are mentioned by ancient writers, among them a *Calumny* (of which Botticelli made a Renaissance version) and an *Aphrodite Anadyomene* (*Aphrodite Rising from the Foam*) later taken to Rome by the emperor Augustus. Apelles was said to excel all other painters in grace and to be a master of chiaroscuro. The *Zeus Enthroned* in the House of the Vetti at Pompeii may be a copy of Apelles' work.

THE ROYAL TOMBS

Excavations at Vergina (Aegae, the ancient Macedonian capital in the hills above Pella) have recently produced remarkable murals. One, possibly from the tomb of Philip II himself and so dating to *c.*338BC, shows a dramatic and complex hunting scene in which for the first time landscape contributes to the picture's depth. The frieze, though much pitted, presents a panoramic view of the hunt, in which the young Alexander is shown on horseback.

Even more vivid is *The Abduction of Persephone*, a mural in a nearby tomb sketched with quick, light strokes that aptly capture the despair of the goddess Demeter. She is shown seated on the right as the shaggy-bearded god Hades carries off her terrified daughter Persephone in his chariot to the underworld. Nicomachus, an artist praised by Pliny, may have created this novel depiction of human emotion.

THE FIRST MOSAICS

Mosaics, that far more laborious and costly, if also far more enduring, form of art than murals or panels, were initially made in pebbles. *Lion Hunt*, dated *c.*320–300BC is from Pella, the

Macedonian capital, and is signed by Gnosis, a famous artist. It depicts two naked youths, one perhaps being Alexander and the other his friend Craterus, who with a hound are attacking a lion. It is a dynamically dramatic scene, the muscular bodies and flying cloaks of the naked hunters and the animals shown with convincing foreshortening and shadowing.

In the Hellenistic and Roman eras, mosaics became commoner and grander, but painted *tesserae* (glass or marble cubes) replaced pebbles. Tesserae were easier to work in than pebbles, which encouraged the spread of mosaics.

Above: The Birth of Venus *from the House of Venus, a mural from Pompeii that probably copies a lost Hellenistic original – a reminder that not all such paintings were masterpieces.*

Below: Botticelli's Calumny of Apelles, *painted in 1495, was a Renaissance attempt to recreate a lost masterpiece by Apelles. Often considered the greatest artist of antiquity, Apelles became Alexander's court painter in the 330s BC.*

THE EVIDENCE OF POMPEII
THE *ALEXANDER MOSAIC*

Above: A detail from the Alexander Mosaic *showing King Darius panic-stricken in his chariot at Alexander's sudden advance.*

Below: The Alexander Mosaic, *the grandest copy of a Greek masterpiece, was made in Pompeii around 100BC. It shows Alexander charging at King Darius. Reproducing a mural probably painted by Apelles c.328BC, it keeps to the original four-colour palette.*

Originally an Etruscan settlement, and so, like many other Etruscan cities, very receptive to Greek culture, Pompeii later became an Oscan town. It prospered on the fertile if, as it finally turned out, perilous lands beneath Mt Vesuvius. Only Romanized properly after Sulla had planted a military colony there in 80BC, Pompeii then expanded further, acquiring a permanent amphitheatre long before Rome did. But at its peak in AD79 its population reached only c.15,000, making it quite small even by the standards of the age.

But there was nothing pettily provincial about Pompeii culturally. It not only had all the trappings of a Graeco-Roman city – temples, baths, a forum, elected officials – it also had long been attracting fine artists from around the Greek world. They produced often excellent copies of renowned Hellenistic paintings that decorated royal palaces in Hellenistic kingdoms such as Pergamum. The quality of the murals and mosaics uncovered at Pompeii and nearby Herculaneum are rivalled only by those excavated from Rome's largest houses and palaces.

THE *ALEXANDER MOSAIC*
Grandest of Pompeian paintings is the *Alexander Mosaic*, the most faithful full-size copy of a Greek masterpiece known. This intensely dramatic battle scene was made for a wealthy – and clearly philhellenic – Pompeian around 100BC and displayed in its own special *exedra* (recess) in his mansion, now called the 'House of the Faun'. The picture shows Alexander powering through the fighting towards his opponent, a terrified King Darius, who is about to flee in his chariot. (Whether the battle shown is the Issus in 333BC or Gaugamela two years later remains debated. The same dramatic incident occurred in both.) The mosaic

in Pompeii reproduces an earlier work that was almost certainly a mural due to the generally free style of its painting.

The mosaic meticulously follows the original work's restricted four-colour palette – red, yellow, black and white – employed by many of the greatest Classical artists from Polygnotus to Apelles. The picture uses highlights, deep-cast shadows and recession in depth to heighten its realism. More recent innovations are the three-dimensional modelling in black (of some of the horses) and the extreme foreshortening of a horse right in the centre, whose rear quarters are seen from behind. The reflected face of a fallen Persian in the burnished shield in the centre marks another advance in dramatic realism.

Very large at 2.7 by 5.1m (8ft 10in by 16ft 9in) and ringing with the tumult of battle, the picture rivals in its emotional impact the grandest works by later Renaissance and Baroque masters. Many archaeologists think that the original was painted by Apelles in *c.*328BC, soon after the battle depicted. Others attribute it to Philoxenos of Eretria, another famous artist of Alexander's age.

THE VILLA AT BOSCOREALE

Very different in tone is the cycle of fresco paintings made *c.*50BC for Publius Fannius Synistor, who owned a large villa at Boscoreale just outside Pompeii. These also copy Hellenistic royal pictures painted nearly 200 years earlier. There are five panels, each with one or two static, almost life-size figures. One shows a craggy philosopher leaning on a stick. In another, a woman personifying Asia is seated looking intensely at a pensive man with a shield opposite her, who has been identified as symbolizing a Macedonian king. Another panel shows a draped women in a gold headband playing a golden cithara, with a girl standing behind her high-backed chair, a contrasting scene of domestic tranquillity. The unknown creator of these pieces was clearly a highly adaptable artist.

Above: A mural from Pompeii of the 1st century BC copying an older Hellenistic work. Depicting the hero Perseus, it shows remarkable illusionistic skills.

Below: This mural of c.50BC from a villa at Pompeii copies a work of c.240BC for a Macedonian royal palace.

THE FINDING OF TELEPHUS

From Herculaneum comes one of the finest paintings of antiquity, a copy of *The Finding of Telephus*. The original was made for Eumenes II of Pergamum in *c.*190BC. Telephus was the son of Hercules. Hercules, flanked by the royal lion and eagle, looks down at his son, being suckled by a doe in the foreground. The boy and deer are masterpieces of tenderly depicted realism. Behind the child sits a female figure personifying Arcadia. She is so majestic, massive and calm that she could have been painted by J.A.D. Ingres (1780–1867), the French Neoclassical master.

IDYLLIC LANDSCAPES
THE GRAECO–ROMAN FUSION

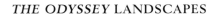

Above: Dionysus riding a panther, a mosaic from a rich merchant's house on Delos made c.120BC.

Below: The great Nile Mosaic *from Praeneste near Rome decorated a public building. It gives a bird's-eye view of the Nile in flood, with temples, boats and animals, copying a Ptolemaic original of c.100BC.*

Landscape painting, seemingly unknown to Classical artists, emerged during the Hellenistic period as often idyllic illustrations of mythical scenes. The genre may have reflected a nostalgia for rural life among people in vast new cities such as Antioch, Alexandria and Rome itself. But it revealed, too, artists' growing skills in suggesting depth and recession, which were at times used to depict cityscapes too. One of the first such scenery painters, generally called *topographoi*, was Demetrius, who worked in Alexandria in the 2nd century BC.

At the Boscoreale Villa near Pompeii the murals of imaginary cities in the main *cubiculum* (bedroom) make superb examples of architectural *trompe l'oeil*. They copy stage scenery from Ephesus painted *c.*150BC and later described by Pliny. Like most original paintings described by writers, the Ephesus works have not survived.

THE ODYSSEY LANDSCAPES
The second more romantic Homeric epic about the wanderings of its homesick hero, *The Odyssey*, was a popular source of stories for painters in the Hellenistic and Roman worlds. (Educated Romans understood Greek.) Unearthed from a house on the Esquiline Hill in Rome in 1848–9, a cycle of eight magnificent murals, painted *c.*50BC but copying earlier Hellenistic work, depicts Odysseus' adventures in sketches done with an almost impressionistic lightness.

The landscapes gain a romantic, indeed menacing air from the huge boulders overshadowing the tiny figures, and from the great vistas of sea and islands opening up beyond them. Such backgrounds add to the drama of the stories. In the first panel Odysseus and his men have innocently arrive in the land of the Laestrygonians. They make inquiries of a graceful woman carrying an amphora descending a path. The tone is pastorally idyllic.

It changes abruptly in the next panels as the Laestrygonians attack Odysseus' men with rocks and trees. The Laestrygonians, who are really cannibals, then destroy many of the Greeks' boats, dragging off the slaughtered Greeks to eat them. Odysseus' ship alone escapes as he sails off with a few companions for Circe's island. Other scenes show Odysseus' descent to the Underworld. The unknown artist radically reduced the size of figures as they recede deeper into the landscape. To identify some of the men dwarfed by the landscape, he helpfully added labels.

THE 'HOUSE OF THE TRAGIC POET'
In the 'House of the Tragic Poet' at Pompeii an unknown painter created a masterpiece in *Achilles and Briseis*, illustrating a scene from *The Iliad*. Achilles smoulders with barely suppressed rage as

Left: From the Villa at Tivoli of the emperor Hadrian (reigned AD117–38) comes this mosaic of drinking doves, a copy of an original made by Sosus of Pergamum in about 150BC. Its realism approaches trompe l'oeil.

Briseis, his favourite slave girl, is forcibly carried off on King Agamemnon's orders. Behind the pitifully weeping figure of Briseis stand a line of threateningly armoured soldiers. The fresco copies a Hellenistic original of *c.*300BC.

In sober, dignified contrast the stucco panel from a villa in Herculaneum shows an exhausted actor resting in his dressing-room. His sceptre and sword indicate that he is playing a royal role. A woman crouches in front of a female tragic mask. (She is not an actress, because men played women's roles in Greek theatre and this painting copies a Greek original of *c.*300BC.) The work may portray the psychological tension between actors' grand roles and their low social status.

MOSAICS EAST AND WEST

The art of mosaic continued to develop, being carried west to Italy. In Delos, booming after Rome made it a tax-free port in 166BC, wealthy Roman or Italian merchants commissioned fine mosaics for their luxurious houses. One of the most striking comes from the 'House of Dionysus', named after its vibrantly coloured mosaic made *c.*120BC. It shows the wine-god on a panther, looking debauched and riding curiously side-saddle. His panther or leopard snarls with feral power, its claws painted with almost alarming realism.

Approximately contemporary is the great *Nile Mosaic* from Praeneste (Palestrina) near Rome made to decorate the apse of a public building. It shows a bird's-eye view of the Nile in flood, with temples, boats, soldiers and animals. Everything is teeming with life and colour. It probably copies a Ptolemaic royal original, but makes no attempt at using perspective.

From the Villa at Tivoli of Hadrian, that most philhellenic of Roman emperors (reigned AD117–38), comes a brilliant copy of a mosaic by Sosus of Pergamum, originally made *c.*150BC. It shows doves drinking from a burnished bowl, whose surface is disturbed by the beak of one sipping bird. This marvel of realism marks the climax of Graeco-Roman cultural fusion as the Roman empire itself passed through its zenith.

Below: From the 'House of the Tragic Poet' at Pompeii comes an anonymous masterpiece illustrating a scene from The Iliad. *It copies a Hellenistic original of* c.300BC.

INDEX